You Shouldn't Join if
You Can't Take a Joke

You Shouldn't Join if You Can't Take a Joke

Ken Kent

ATHENA PRESS
LONDON

ISBN 978 1 84748 668 4

First published by Avon Books 2006
This edition published 2009 by
ATHENA PRESS
Queen's House, 2 Holly Road
Twickenham TW1 4EG
United Kingdom

Printed for Athena Press

I dedicate this book to all the shipmates who served with me,
without whom this volume would not be possible,
and to my dear wife, Sylvia, who spent many hours proofreading it.

Contents

1
HMS Ganges
(Shotley)

What does a young lad of the tender age of fifteen want from life? At that age, the desire to drive a train or play football or cricket for England has diminished with the passage of time, but it is unlikely that anything really feasible has been decided upon.

It came, therefore, as something as a surprise and a shock when, just after my fifteenth birthday, my mother suddenly asked me if I would like to join the Navy. I was nonplussed at the time. I had never had any desire to be a sailor and the thought of climbing up high masts and performing on yardarms was, to say the least, slightly disconcerting. I was more or less content with my lot. I was studying at a secondary school, doing quite well with two languages and did have a faint hope of becoming an interpreter. Then there was Cyril Hunter, my inseparable companion, with whom I spent many happy hours in our leisure time, and to be suddenly whisked away from all this took a bit of thinking about.

By dint of gentle persuasion and favourable reports from an ex-naval friend of my mother's, and the fact that she was only earning thirty shillings a week and not in receipt of a widow's pension, I eventually found myself on a train bound for Manchester, my destination being the RN & RM recruiting office in order to receive a medical examination and an educational test. Here I must say that this was the only proper medical examination I ever had during the whole of my naval life. The education test was quite simple and posed no problems. After a brief wait, I was pronounced fit and was duly accepted and told to go back home to await my summons to join up.

Some three months later, on 20 November 1935, I was again en route to Manchester with orders to report once more to the recruiting office. Along with some more apprehensive-looking lads, I was subjected to another medical exam and educational test and then given some cash and directed to a boarding house in which to spend the night, prior to joining our train the next day. I quite enjoyed the evening, with a visit to a well-known cinema and a chance to listen to one of my favourite broadcasting organists. I must admit that I didn't sleep very well and was glad to report to the recruiting office at 0830, ready for the big adventure.

We were all issued with a train ticket to Harwich, a 'pass for recruits', which contained a description of ourselves (to prevent improper use being made of the pass) and a request to all police authorities, railway officials and officers of steamers to assist us if, by accident, we should miss our passage, and a typewritten document with explicit instructions on how to proceed from Manchester to Harwich. We were ushered to the station by the recruiting chief, in order that he may see us safely on our way, thus relieving him of his responsibilities.

I don't remember much about the journey except climbing off a boat that had brought us from Harwich onto the pier at Shotley. This was our destination. Shotley, on which perched HMS *Ganges*, was situated on a peninsular jutting out into Harwich harbour and was prey to the most bitter winds that ever blew off the North Sea.

HMS *Ganges* was a naval barracks built for the sole purpose for training boys of fifteen years upwards, staffed by chief and petty officers as our instructors, and Royal Marines (known as 'Jocks' or 'Bootnecks'), who carried out most of the other tasks. Our first day was mostly concerned with showers, getting kitted out, medical and dental inspections, drawing bedding (two blankets and a pillow), and settling in the mess. We were then acquainted with the rules and regulations, the strictest of which was that we mustn't smoke. In order that this rule was most strictly observed, there was a squad of marines whose sole job was to act as a sort of Gestapo with the purpose of bringing any boy caught smoking to justice, which took the form of seven days' 'jankers' for the first offence. No mercy was ever shown. Another part of our initiation was the visit to the barber's shop. To this we were marched, and then we fell in outside and ushered in two at a time. The first two disappeared inside and reappeared within about two minutes bearing expressions of horror, and in response to our queries removed their caps to confront us with the sight of two Kojak lookalikes.

'Why didn't you ask for a light trim?' someone asked.

'You must be joking!' one of them replied. 'There's two bloody great marines in there, and all they have is a pair of electric shears apiece and they start at the front and go right over the top of your head. When my girlfriend sees this, she won't want to know!'

When we had all been similarly shorn, we were told to 'get fell in' and were marched to the swimming baths and handed over to the tender mercies of a mean-looking PTI (physical training instructor). The swimming baths were in a formidable building situated right down on the foreshore. Hanging on some clothes lines were a number of white duck suits or, as the weather was freezing, it would be more correct to say hooked over the lines, as the suits were frozen solid.

'Right then,' said the PTI, 'all those who can swim, get into your swimming gear and then put the duck suit on.' We found that the only way to accomplish this was by dipping the suits in the swimming bath, which thawed them out sufficiently for us to be able to put them on.

When we were thus attired, the PTI said, 'Off you go, then! Dive in, swim two lengths, then take the suit off at the deep end while still in the water.'

After we had done our two lengths and completed the 'Houdini' act (with a certain amount of difficulty), it was the turn of the non-swimmers. They were all stood in a row on the edge of the bath at the deep end when the PTI – quick as a flash – ran along the row and shoved them all in the water. There was a frantic thrashing of arms and legs, shouts of alarm and frantic efforts to grab hold of the rail at the side of the bath… After they had all clambered out, the PTI announced, 'Now you know what it's like to be thrown into the water and not be able to swim, and if you ever fell overboard at sea you'd drown for certain!'

Our next objective was the parade ground for our initiation into the delights of marching and drilling, and on arrival there we were greeted with the sight of the tallest mast we had ever seen looming overhead. As we craned our necks to look up at the dizzy heights, the instructor said, 'That's right, lads, get a good look at it. You'll be going over the top of that before you're very much older.'

Our joining routine carried on until finally came the dreaded moment. Our chief said, 'Right lads, here's the time you've all been waiting for,' and marched us off to the foot of the mast. It was not much consolation to know that there was a very large safety net suspended about twelve feet above the ground when you were informed that the height of this monster was 140 feet, and that in order to qualify for leave we had to get up to the top and down again in three minutes.

About fifty feet up, there was a type of platform, and there were two ways of arriving on it. One was straight up the rigging through what was known as the lubber's hole, and the other was up the futtock shrouds up the outside. We were not allowed to go through the lubber's hole. Naturally, the first set of climbers stopped on arrival at the futtock shrouds as it meant hanging backwards to get over them, whereupon the chief, bearing in his hand a broomstick on which a large needle was fastened, came clambering up the rigging and started jabbing the luckless climbers up the backside with this awesome weapon. Needless to say, they didn't linger much longer, and were soon on their merry way up into the clouds. A bit brutal perhaps, but it overcame everyone's fear of heights, and probably a few punctured buttocks made it worth it.

For the first six months of our service life, we were known as second-class boys or 'nozzers' and our pay was five shillings and nine pence a week (about twenty-eight pence in the currency of today.) Of this we were coerced into sending our parents the sum of 2s 6d (half a crown), leaving 3s 3d. Every Wednesday the whole lot of us were fallen in on the parade ground, and as our names were called we had to double up to the pay table, remove our cap, place it crown uppermost on the table and recite our ship's book number, upon which the paymaster would deposit one shilling on the aforementioned headgear, followed by, 'About turn, double march!' The balance was placed in our 'credit' from which was deducted any expenses we might incur, such as clothing and so on.

After six months, we were made first-class boys, our pay was increased to 8s 9d (forty-three pence) and we received the munificent sum of an extra sixpence on our caps on Wednesday afternoons. As well as becoming first-class boys, we had to decide in which branch of the service we wished to serve, either gunnery, torpedoes (which also at that time embraced electrics) or communications.

As I have mentioned, probably the most serious crime at Shotley was to be caught smoking. There were no cautions or pardons. The first offence meant seven days' jankers. This meant doubling round the parade ground for an hour every evening bearing a 'janker pole' (about the size of a broomstick, only thicker and heavier). Every now and again the order was given, 'Poles above your heads!' and the pole was then raised up to the full extent of the arms. The speed at which the said offenders doubled was, naturally, the absolute minimum and was known as the 'Shotley shuffle', and although the supervising PO kept spurring his charges on for a bit more effort, the pace was imperceptibly reduced until the Shotley shuffle was once more achieved.

It seemed very difficult to find a place to have a furtive smoke without being detected by the jocks and being hauled off to face justice. The heads (latrines) were not much use. You couldn't shut the door and light up because all the doors had been removed, so that every act of nature was performed in full view of anyone who happened upon the scene.

At first there did seem to be one loophole through which the smokers could achieve their furtive wishes, and that was on what was laughingly known as 'Shotley leave'. This was granted on Sunday afternoons when the boys were permitted to walk up the road outside the main gate for a distance of about half a mile. There was a village grocery shop on the route which no doubt sold fags and matches. Come Sunday afternoon, we saw them depart hopefully through the gates in anticipation of a quiet and undetected drag. It did not seem very long before a disappointed and dejected bunch of malcontents shuffled back through the gates. When I asked one of them how he fared, he replied, 'We hadn't a hope in hell. The road was swarming with jocks, hiding behind hedges and trees. We just wasted our bloody time, and the shop was shut. Never again!'

The barracks was divided into divisions, which bore the names of such illustrious heroes as Benbow, Anson, Collingwood and Hawke. This was done to try to promote a competitive spirit between the boys, so that they would become proud of their respective divisions. I don't seem to remember much enthusiasm among the lads to achieve any outstanding feats in order to demonstrate a superiority over their rival divisions. Probably it was because the competitions in which we took part were not so much football or cricket but boring items such as flag hoisting competitions, gunnery practice drills and, most obnoxious of all, the obstacle cutter races.

A cutter is a large, heavy, unwieldy boat that is propelled by two masts and sails or twelve oars. The idea of the race was row half a mile, up masts and sails then sail a half-mile, down mast and sails, out oars and row half a mile, ad infinitum. The divisional officer of the Hawke Division had an obsession. It seemed to be his one aim in life that Hawke Division was not only going to win the obstacle cutters but also shatter every record that had ever been set, so every minute of their spare time saw the Hawkes 'messing about in boats', as the saying goes; only they were not messing about. They were grafting their guts out! Hail, rain or shine made no difference. The man showed no mercy. Poor devils, they had our full sympathy.

Came the great day of the races and the few who were interested, plus some who were no doubt pressed, went down to witness the event. Naturally every Hawke cutter won by a mile. Their weeks of training – plus the fact that none of us were prepared to slog our guts out unnecessarily when we knew we had no chance – were contributory factors. Anyway, we had heard a rumour that their failure would be rewarded with jankers, so who were we to be the instruments of inflicting unjust punishment on these poor unfortunates? They had suffered enough already.

On becoming first-class boys we also had to decide in which

branch we would spend the rest of our time in the service. Initially I rather fancied being a wireless operator but found that I could read Morse better by sight than by ear, so I became a visual signalman, or signal boy as the case may be. Thus most of our time was spent reading Morse and semaphore, learning vast amounts of rigmarole on all aspects of fleet signalling and manoeuvring, periods in the schoolroom learning navigation plus a bit of English and maths, and the inevitable drilling and marching.

Wednesday was the best day of the week because, as well as being paid, there was 'make and mend' (afternoon off), and in the evening a film was shown in the gymnasium, plus the inevitable *Tom and Jerry*. In addition to these attractions, we had what is known at the present time as a singalong – but with a difference. There must have been a certain amount of lyrical talent among the ship's company because our renditions consisted of parodies of the hits of the day with reference to life at Shotley. I still remember two. One was 'Empty saddles in the old corral' which was parodied as 'Empty cutters at the old pierhead, where are the Hawkes tonight?' There was one I wrote myself, changing 'She was sweet sixteen, little Angeline, always dancing on the village green' into 'He was sweet sixteen, little Jimmy Green, always dragging in the field latrine.' We were accompanied by members of the marine band who didn't seem to enjoy it much, which made it all the more enjoyable for us. They weren't all that popular.

Another form of entertainment was provided by the Methodist chaplain, who was a much respected and well-liked figure of the community. The Rev. Owen Roebuck possessed a cine projector and used to show cartoons and Laurel and Hardy films in the recreation space for his congregation and others who became Methodists for the evening.

Ours was a healthy life, with plenty of outdoor activity, which had the effect of creating a state of permanent hunger. Our meals never seemed to be big enough, and although they were, to all intents and purposes, quite adequate and always well cooked, the pangs of hunger still remained. This meant that our letters to our parents contained continued requests for food parcels. One of the lads whose parents were not very well endowed with cash even wrote home and asked if they could manage some bread and jam sandwiches. When any parcels arrived, the boy concerned was piped for, to report to the mail office where his parcel was opened by a petty officer and diligently searched to ensure that no cigarettes had been smuggled in among the foodstuffs.

Life slowly dragged on. Each day was ticked off on home-made calendars indicating the number of days to leave. This was always a joyous occasion. We were taken to the railway station in a fleet of buses and on arrival there was a mad dash to buy fags and matches (mostly Woodbines) from the kiosk and from a heavily laden trolley filled with chocolates and cigarettes, which someone had had the presence of mind to provide in addition, so that we may all be provided for, before the train departed bearing its joyous load. Within minutes of boarding, it appeared as though there was more smoke coming out of the carriage windows than out of the locomotive's funnel! I still remember the words of a song that was popular during that Christmas leave, and they went, 'I'm going home for Christmas, can you wonder why I'm glad?' Never was a song sung with more feeling.

The last calendar to be ticked off was the one that denoted the end of our time in *Ganges*. When this great day arrived, we were divided up geographically, some to Chatham, some to Portsmouth and the rest to Plymouth, depending how close you lived to these respective destinations. I suppose Chatham is fractionally nearer to Hull than Portsmouth, with the result that all of us in the Hull contingent found ourselves bound for Chatham on 5 February 1937.

2
HMS Pembroke
(Chatham Barracks)

C hatham is one of the three Medway towns, and the barracks
are situated at the bottom of a long hill next to the dockyard.
It is not a very large town and not a lot happens there. There was
one consolation, however, as far as I was concerned, and that was
the fact that the building of two new super cinemas was nearing
completion which, at the age of sixteen, was a delight to be
savoured to the full. In those days it was the custom to show two
feature films plus a newsreel in addition to my favourite item,
about half an hour of organ music played on a 'Mighty Wurlitzer'.

On arrival at the barracks, we were marched to our living
quarters, given about half an hour to stow our gear, then told to
fall in, in order to be instructed in the routine of acquiring our
cards. A card might not seem much to the ordinary person, but to
a matelot in barracks it is a vital possession. It has to be surrendered before going on leave (no card – no leave) and is a kind of
internal passport. Nearly every activity or item drawn from stores
cannot be accomplished without the production of the card. To
acquire this precious document is almost an art form in itself. It
was not really a card but a small handbook of about six pages, and
on being issued in its blank form had to be stamped by every
department and officer in the establishment, such as the medical
officer, the dental officer, the pay office, the victualling office –
you name it, they stamped it. Naturally, with a large intake of
boys, it meant queuing up at every visit and the whole procedure
took about two days. In later life in the service we came to realise
that here was a good chance for a skive, and the joining routine
could be made to last out for three or four days; in fact, I knew of
one old salt who boasted that he spun it out over two weeks.

The only part of this routine that was not too pleasant was the visit to the gas-mask depot. On being issued with gas masks and having our cards duly stamped, we then had to test the masks. This entailed entering a brick building with no windows and only one door with our masks on. This building was full of tear gas, and once inside we had to stand for a minute or two and then, on the command of the instructor, remove our masks and walk slowly out of the building. We were informed that this was done to prove that we had been in a gas-filled chamber. We would have been quite prepared to take his word for it.

Chatham life was completely different to that at Shotley. There was no set routine of drilling or marching, no Morse or semaphore to read, and no classes for the advancement of our knowledge of signals. All that seemed to be provided for signal ratings was a room up in the top of the drill shed building in which people used to sit all day and spin yarns.

We were given leave from one o'clock on Saturday afternoons, and we now received the whole of our pay less the allotments that were stopped out of it. Things were looking up. Compared with the spartan life in *Ganges*, this was heaven. My Saturdays ashore then consisted of a film show for sixpence (2½p), a high tea of fish and chips in Woolworth's, or bangers and mash in the local café for four or five pence (2p), followed by a visit to a theatre to see a variety show – another sixpence. So my whole day out only cost the equivalent of ten pence in present-day currency, and I always thoroughly enjoyed it.

Outside the drafting office in the drill shed there was a large noticeboard which was scrutinised daily by nearly everyone to see whether or not they had got a 'draft chit' – in other words, a posting to a ship – and though I and my friends from Shotley went down there daily, we always seemed to draw a blank. We were beginning to wonder if we would forget how to read Morse and semaphore. We hadn't joined to sit in a smoke-filled loft above the drill shed all day listening to old matelots' yarns. The novelty of having an easy life was wearing a bit thin. Boredom was beginning to creep in when one day a shout went up, 'They're commissioning the *Warspite* at Pompey and there's hundreds of names on the drafting board!'

We all went rushing down and, sure enough, there were our

names with the instructions to have our kitbags and hammocks packed and outside the mess by 0800 on 29 June 1937.

The following morning saw us ready to depart when a number of lorries rolled up. In went our bags and hammocks and then we were marched down to the dockyard, where we were amazed to see a passenger train waiting to take us on our journey. The lorries arrived from the barracks and we proceeded to load our bags and hammocks into some covered wagons and then boarded the train ourselves. We were expecting to have to change at Victoria and Waterloo, as is the case when travelling under normal circumstances. We were, however, delighted when we kept rolling along and realised that somehow Southern Railways had the necessary expertise to transport us from Kent to Hampshire without the toil of transferring both ourselves and our kit from one train to another.

We finally arrived at Pitch House Jetty, Portsmouth Dockyard, and gazed up in awe at this mighty battleship. It was the first time us lads had ever seen a warship 'in the flesh' as it were, and the thought of being part of this massive fighting machine was tinged with a certain amount of speculative anticipation.

3
HMS Warspite

The name '*Warspite*' goes back to the time of Elizabeth I. In fact, *Warspite* was the name of Sir Walter Raleigh's Flagship. The present-day version is a nuclear submarine. The vessel in which I received my baptism by sea was commissioned in March 1915 and fought in the battle of Jutland. Unfortunately, during this encounter her steering jammed in the midst of battle and she commenced turning circles within range of the enemy guns. Naturally the Germans were not slow to take advantage of such a gift and concentrated their fire on this unfortunate ship. All credit must be given to British workmanship because she sustained twenty-nine direct hits by enemy shells before the steering fault was corrected and she was able to steam back to port without assistance.

She was a mighty battleship of 36,000 tons with a main armament of eight fifteen-inch guns, capable of firing a one ton shell a distance of over ten miles. Also there were eight six-inch guns and sundry anti-aircraft weapons.

In 1934 she was sent to Portsmouth to be completely refitted. This was an enormous task and resulted in the old ship being almost stripped down to just the hull to accommodate the replacement of the boilers and turbines. The fighting top was scrapped altogether and replaced by a modern superstructure. The mainmast was replaced by a smaller one and the foremast became the predominant feature. This was a huge affair with a ladder that went right up the inside as far as the crosstrees.

The refit was completed in March 1937 and on the eighth she sailed for trials, but all was not well. While carrying out a full power steering trial, the helm jammed at hard a-starboard, despite having a new steering engine fitted. The curse of Jutland was rearing its ugly head once more. So it was back to the drawing board or, in this case, back to the dockyard, for the necessary remedial work. She was supposed to sail for the Mediterranean in July but these hopes were dashed. The problem of the jammed helm seemed insurmountable, and it was only after weeks of trials and dockings that it was calculated that the trouble was being caused by interaction between the inner and outer propellers. The only way to overcome this problem was to decrease speed on the outer shafts when turning at more than 200 rpm.

She was finally handed over from the dockyard staff on 27 June and pronounced fit to receive the rest of the ship's company to bring her up to her full complement of 1,218 officers and men, and we all duly arrived on 29 June.

With much anticipation we boarded the ship and went through the process of settling in. We stowed our bags and hammocks, familiarised ourselves with the layout of the ship and met the senior ratings of our respective branches, who informed us of the ship's routine and what our duties would be. Things didn't seem too bad. The boys' mess deck was quite adequate for our needs, the work didn't seem too arduous and there was shore leave in Portsmouth, which seemed to have more to offer than Chatham.

Then the blow fell. We were introduced to our divisional officer, who turned out to be none other than the obstacle cutter fanatic from Shotley. Having made Hawke division the best at *Ganges*, he was now going to make the *Warspite* boys division the finest in the Navy! We were about fifty strong and were divided up into separate divisions to try to promote a competitive spirit (will they never learn?), and a large chart was stuck up on the noticeboard on which points were added for such things as giving a smart salute, being smartly turned out and so on, and having your points deducted for cap not on straight, being in need of a haircut, or the polish on your boots not being up to regulation brilliance and similar idiotic misdemeanours. He actually donated a trophy to spur us on to greater efforts. I'm sure the opposite applied. To win that trophy would be a matter for eternal shame. The word 'creepers' would have sprung to mind...

Thankfully there were no cutters on board but unfortunately there was a whaler; this is smaller than a cutter, having only five oars and masts and sails. There was much speculation as to how long it would be before the lads were doing their galley slave impersonations. Luckily, signal boys and boy telegraphists were not permitted to indulge in such pursuits, for which we were more than grateful. We had duties of our own which precluded us from participating in these delights. Naturally, it wasn't long before the leading hand was told to detail off some volunteers to sample the doubtful pleasures of rowing and sailing to and fro across Portsmouth Harbour.

Another indignity that was heaped upon us was the hammock lashing ritual. For those unacquainted with the stowage of a naval hammock. I will explain. It is made of stout canvas and contains a mattress, pillow and blanket. On turning out in the morning the blanket is folded up inside with the pillow and the whole lot is then bound round with a length of rope known as a 'hammock lashing' (which is the same thickness as an ordinary household clothes line), so that it finishes up in the shape of a large sausage. In order to ensure that they were properly lashed up in a seaman-like fashion, we had to take them up onto the upper deck. Here, the duty leading hand was waiting for us holding a hoop with a radius of about two feet. The hammock had then to be passed through the hoop, and if it failed to do so the culprit was sentenced to extra hammock lashing drill in his own time in the dog watches and also had five points deducted off the wall chart.

Next came the boys' boxing spectacular. We were fallen in in two ranks, shortest on the right, tallest on the left, and paired off in like sizes. We were then informed that a boxing tournament had been arranged for the entertainment of the officers and the ship's company, and that we should all box three rounds with the boy with whom we had been paired.

A boxing ring was rigged up in the hangar and seats brought in for the officers (naturally). The rest had to stand. The lad I drew, although being the same height as me, was about two stone heavier, and in fact he was the only boy in the Navy who had permission to grow a beard. I think his name was Harry Wicks. He was quite a decent sort of lad but he knocked seven bells out of me. I wish I'd had the same good sense as Joe Miles. Joe Miles said, 'I'm not going to get knocked around for three rounds just to entertain those sadistic bleeders. I'm going to take a dive!'

When his turn came, he sparred for a few seconds and as soon as his opponent landed a blow he dropped to the canvas as though poleaxed and lay there prone. Despite the blandishments of the PTI, such as, 'Get up and box, you skiving bastard!' he lay there prone until counted out. Then he got up and departed from the hangar, to the accompaniment of boos from the ship's company and cheers from the boys.

The furious divisional officer said, 'I'll teach you a lesson!' and deducted a whole ten points off his chart. Joe lost a lot of sleep over that!

Life dragged on. Two of the lads who had joined up with me, Eric Collier and Phil Robinson, volunteered to join the Fleet Air Arm as Telegraphist Air Gunners. I heard that Eric Collier got killed in the war, but Phil Robby was more fortunate and finished up as station commander at one of the Fleet Air Arm shore bases. At least, that's what he told me when I saw him many years later.

Then, one wet and windy Saturday afternoon, I was duty messenger and had a signal for the Commander, whom I tracked down in the wardroom. He was standing near a porthole when I gave him it.

He read it and then glanced out of the porthole and said, 'Who the hell's got a whaler out on a day like this?'

'We have, sir,' I replied, trying to hide the satisfaction in my voice that someone was going to get his comeuppance. 'It's a crew from the boys' mess deck, sir,' I said, turning the knife.

'Right,' he ordered, 'send the leading hand of the boys' mess deck to me at once.'

Naturally no one heard the conversation, but the killick poured his heart out about the indignities we had to suffer and the way that this man was creating a miserable existence for boys and those in charge.

It was during the following week that the killick (leading seaman) burst upon the mess deck whooping excitedly.

'He's gone – the bugger's gone!' he yelled. He rushed across to the noticeboard and ripped the chart into little pieces, whereupon the other killick grabbed the trophy, rushed up on to the upper deck and hurled as far as he could into the depths of Pompey

Harbour. We were liberated! The tyrant had been given his marching orders, and we were thankful that our Commander had shown such humane feelings.

Some days later, a wardroom messenger came down to the mess deck in search of a trophy which had been requested to be forwarded on. Funnily, no one seemed to have any knowledge of its whereabouts. The messenger returned empty-handed.

The boys were not the only ones who seemed to be having troubles. A number of the ship's company thought they were being unfairly treated as regards weekend leave. A large proportion lived in the Chatham area and weekend leave expired at 0700 on Monday mornings. The train times were so arranged by Southern Rail that, to be back on board in time, they had to leave home at 2200 (10 p.m.) on Sunday night. Quite a lot of resentment built up, and what with living under the feet of dockyard workmen and trying to get the ship into seagoing condition, plus endless trials, things finally came to a head. It was therefore decided to hold a meeting in the mess deck.

This came to the ears of the officer of the watch, who duly informed the Captain, who immediately cleared lower deck and defused the situation by listening to the grievances and then pointing out the proper manner in which to state a complaint through the official channels. He then reported the matter to the C.-in-C. who decided to let the matter drop, but unfortunately a popular daily newspaper got to hear and published an article with dark hints of mutiny and blew the thing up out of all proportion (as you would expect). Naturally, the Admiralty got to hear and ordered an official enquiry, with the result that three officers were relieved of their appointments, three ratings were discharged from the service and nine drafted to other ships. The gutter press triumphed again.

Each time we went ashore on leave we had to pass Nelson's flagship, the *Victory*. Being young lads, the significance that Nelson was the most brilliant and courageous admiral who ever lived was lost on us. In fact, he used to take the blame for a lot of the tradition and 'bull' that existed in the RN, and it never entered our heads to go and inspect the ship where this great man achieved such glory. It wasn't until many years later, after I had left the service and was on holiday in Southsea, that I visited the ship. Of course, by then, being more mature I had read a number of books on the Napoleonic sea battles and was anxious to complete my knowledge and visit the ship of the great man.

Luckily our guide was a matelot with a very dry sense of humour and one of the stories with which he regaled us was of the methods used for boarding enemy vessels after lying along-side. He said that the enemy used to swing across from one vessel to the other on ropes in the rigging. The crew of the *Victory* would be waiting to greet them armed with long, sharply pointed poles on which they spiked the enemy as they swung across the intervening gap. Those who spiked the most bodies were picked for the ship's darts team.

We next went down below to view the mess decks. Hanging over each mess table were short lengths of rope decorated with fancy knots such as Turk's head and so on, and on being asked the purpose of these we were told that in those days there were no knives or forks as such and all food was mainly eaten with the fingers. The ropes were there for the crew to wipe their fingers on so they became impregnated with meat juices, gravy and such. He then went on to say (tongue in cheek) that once a week the cooks took these ropes down and boiled them in water, thus providing the crew with a bowl of soup each. I somehow don't think these are extracts from the guidebook but they did add enjoyment to a memorable visit and our thanks went out to that 'Jolly Jack Tar'.

At long last the dockyard work and trials were completed and we set sail for the Mediterranean on 5 January 1938, some 5½ months late. The Bay of Biscay was in an ugly mood and there was a large number of the ship's company being very sick and wishing they were dead. Fortunately I am a good sailor, and have never been seasick, therefore when the weather was a bit rough there was always plenty of spare food going. Big eats, as they say.

We arrived in Malta on 14 January and took up our berth in Grand Harbour as the flagship of a very powerful fleet. Moored astern were the battleships *Barham* and *Malaya*; in Bighi Bay were the *Hood* and *Renown*, in Corredeno Creek was the first cruiser squadron (Arethusa Class); and in Canteen Creek the second cruiser squadron (County class). In Sliema harbour were three flotillas of destroyers (twenty-seven boats) plus the Rear Admiral (Destroyers) in a cruiser.

On 6 February, Admiral Sir Dudley Pound, C.-in-C. Mediterranean, hoisted his flag in *Warspite*. Then, after inspecting the ship's company, he gave us all a thorough dressing-down for what he called our mutinous behaviour in Portsmouth. We all thought this a bit of a green rub, as the people responsible for these admonitions had all left the ship. Official chroniclers have remarked that this only spurred the crew on to prove that he was wrong in his opinion. I personally don't recall any sudden upsurge of enthusiasm to bear this out. It was more likely that 'He doesn't know what he's talking about and carry on regardless,' was in our minds at the time.

It seemed that the occupation of the entire population of Malta was tending to the needs of the Mediterranean fleet. There must have been about 40,000 or more officers and men to cater for and they seemed to cope quite adequately. There were more bars than it was possible to count. In Valetta there was the world-famous street, Statta Stretta, known to all as 'the Gut', which consisted solely of bars, cabarets, eating houses and places where you could get a bed for the night for a shilling. A cabaret was merely a bar that employed a pianist and a dancer or two. Most bars had 'hostesses' (I use the term very loosely), better known to us as sherry girls. They would come and sit down at your table and say, 'You buy me sherry, Jack,' to which the standard reply would be 'Piss off,' or words to that effect. Incidentally, the 'sherry' was a small tot of cherryade or Vimto. I don't recall seeing much sherry behind the bars in the Gut.

One of the unique features of Malta is the type of boat peculiar to the island known as a *dghaisa*. On first encountering them, it appears very strange to see the oarsman standing up, facing forward and pushing the oars. The service pronunciation was 'diso' and every boatman was called Joe. In fact, every native of every foreign port was called Joe by every matelot, whether he was a barman, taxi driver, shopkeeper or *ghari* driver. All answered to the name of Joe.

There was always a small flotilla of *dghaisas* lying off each ship, waiting to ferry anyone ashore or to another ship. Similarly, every landing point on shore had a few waiting for those wishing to make the return journey. The price never varied. It was always sixpence.

The imagination needed in choosing meals ashore was zero. I never ever remember anyone asking for anything other than egg and chips. When sitting in a bar and suddenly feeling the pangs of hunger it was merely enough to shout, 'Egg and chips, Joe!' or 'Big eats, Joe!' It then seemed as if a jungle telegraph went into operation because within a very short space of time a body would appear with a lump of rope round his neck, one end of which was attached a Primus stove with a frying pan at the other.

Within minutes the required victuals would be sizzling away in the pan while Joe squatted down pumping away at his Primus stove. I don't ever remember seeing where the victuals came from – probably loose in his pockets – or who provided the plates, knives and forks. This didn't detract from the taste, and anyway, when you'd had a few bottles of Blue Label you weren't really bothered.

Many pages could be devoted to our exploits during runs ashore in Malta, but we weren't out there for that. The most important thing was getting the ship moulded into an efficient fighting unit. This entailed many exercises in all aspects of seamanship, and, most important, bringing the efficiency of the gun crews up to the highest standard. We, as signal staff, were not at all keen on this. The flag deck was very close to those mighty fifteen-inch gun turrets. The detonation from these weapons is quite tremendous, and stuffing our ears up with cotton wool was not the slightest bit of use. When the first salvo was fired, an enormous amount of soot flew out of the funnel and settled on the upper deck and all the poor unfortunates on it. We all resembled refugees from the Black and White Minstrels. As we were the fleet flagship, we had to be the best of all, and so these exercises and gunnery practices dragged on and on. Finally we achieved the required standard and the time arrived for 'showing the flag'.

We set sail from Malta and, after a couple of days' steaming, arrived at Corfu. According to the present-day tour operators,

Corfu is an ideal place to spend a couple of weeks on holiday. It was a different story in the 1930s. It was a pretty desolate spot for a run ashore. The bars and the beer were definitely not up to scratch, and I seem to recollect that we drank vermouth, which was about a shilling a bottle.

On top of all this, we were lumbered with an official visit from the King of Greece. Every inch of paintwork had to be washed down. Every inch of deck (upper and lower) had to be scrubbed, everything that needed polishing was polished and repolished, and anything that showed the slightest blemish was painted. There wasn't a spare inch of that ship that remained untouched. We wouldn't have minded, but the ship was always kept spotlessly clean in the normal course of events.

Came the day and the royal party arrived. We were all fell in in our respective divisions (no one excused) on the upper deck, and had to stand there waiting to be inspected by His Royal Highness, Dudley Pound and all their hangers-on. They then retired to a dais on the quarterdeck and we had to march past in single file to the accompaniment of the bootnecks' band.

There were also visits to similar uninteresting places, where the speculation was that Dudley Pound was there for the duck shooting but that was probably only a matelots' 'buzz'. After pottering round the eastern end of the Mediterranean, we finally returned to Malta. Christmas came and went with the usual festivities, and then it was time for the spring manoeuvres.

The spring manoeuvres were preceded by the Mediterranean Fleet and the Home Fleet all gathering together in Gibraltar. They would be divided into two fleets, the red fleet and the blue fleet, and would then sail out into the Atlantic and fight mock battles and carry out manoeuvres and exercises. This was done from Monday to Friday on three successive weeks. This was always regarded as good fun by those in high places, but we of the lower deck were totally bored by the whole proceedings and couldn't wait to get back into Gibraltar harbour and get ashore.

One of the features of the shore facilities in Gibraltar was a strangely constructed toilet block in the dockyard. There were the usual cubicles containing toilet seats but the flushing arrangements were slightly different. Underneath the seats was a large trough that ran the full length of the seats and at one end there was a cistern that operated every few minutes, providing a flow of water which carried away the accumulated droppings into a sump at the other end. This was a heaven-sent opportunity for the practical jokers who would occupy the end toilet under the cistern, take a newspaper, construct a large ball of paper, then, as the cistern flushed, float it on the water and set it alight with a match, thus providing a few unfortunate sailors with singed backsides.

However, there was some icing on the cake. After three weeks of ploughing the ocean, every ship sailed for some exotic port to recuperate and, being the flagship, we anchored at Villefranche, midway between Nice and Monte Carlo. We had been unaware that we would ever stay at such an earthly paradise, and consequently had not made the necessary provisions as regards cash. We should have saved up, but only having a few shillings in our pockets we were not able to take full advantage of all the goodies on offer, or some of the more exotic French cuisine. We didn't have egg and chips, though; it was '*oeuf et la pomme de terre*'. I seem to remember visiting a cinema in Nice showing English films, which I believe was called the King Edward VII, and we were nonplussed when the usherette wanted a tip for showing us to our seats. I'm afraid one of the more uncouth members of the party gave her the 'sherry girl' salutation. I think she got the message.

All good things must come to an end, and so it was with much reluctance that we set off back to Malta for the more mundane things of life.

The next state visit was to Alexandria, to entertain the King of Egypt. He was only a young fellow of about eighteen at the time and didn't want a lot of palaver and ceremony (a lad after our own hearts). All he wanted was to go to sea and see the big fifteen-inch guns fired, and furthermore he wanted a full broadside. This is not normally recommended, as it throws too much strain on the ship's structure, but as it was a royal request, so be it. Off we went to sea, bearing the young monarch and his followers. We had hoped that he would bring the young Queen Farina with him, as she was greatly admired, but our hopes were unfulfilled. We reached the appropriate spot in the ocean and opened fire. It was like the crack of doom. The ship gave a mighty lurch and the massive wads of cotton wool that we stuffed in our ears had not the slightest effect. The funnel belched out its usual load of thick black soot, while down below the cork chippings which were part of the decoration on the deckheads (ceilings) in the mess decks rained down on all and sundry. Although Farouk seemed to enjoy it, his entourage were not of the same mind and all disappeared below decks like startled rabbits down a hole.

The shooting finally finished and we returned to Alexandria which, being a city of some considerable size, was a fairly decent place for a run ashore. I remember seeing *Carmen Miranda* at the Mohamed Ali Cinema, and also a film that was shown on TV only the other day, namely *Scrooge* with Seymour Hicks. There were a few bars and cabarets but not up to the standard of those in Malta, and certainly not as cheap, so we weren't sorry to be back there after visiting some rather uninteresting places on the return journey.

My early years at a secondary school, it appears, were not entirely wasted, as I was able to pass some educational exams. This entitled me to be promoted from boy signalman to ordinary signalman at the age of seventeen and a half instead of eighteen, with a subsequent pay rise from eight and nine pence per week to 14s (70p). Nine months later came the upgrading to signalman at 21s per week (£1.05). At last I was earning a decent wage! The next step up the ladder was that of trained operator, which merely meant an ability to read Morse and semaphore at the very highest speed possible. This also carried an added bonus of an extra three pence per day. There was a small signal school ashore where it was possible to do the necessary course in order to achieve these skills, so I applied and in due course was accepted and spent quite a few pleasant days on shore. The speed tests were not too bad, and, after all, we had been reading Morse and semaphore for well over two years. Another reason for wanting to become a trained operator was the fact that signalmen could not be accepted for service in destroyers unless they bore this rank, and I had been getting a bit disgruntled with the spit and polish of a fleet flagship and fancied the free and easy lifestyle of destroyers. As soon as I was rated TO, I put in for a transfer to the destroyer service, and was informed that I could go as soon as a vacancy arose.

It was about the middle of 1938 that Hitler was stirring the pot in Europe and helping himself to other people's countries, and as the crisis boiled up, Their Lordships decided that it might be prudent for the fleet to be loaded with live ammunition instead of practice shells. The order was then issued for all ships to signal their requirements to the ammunition ship lying in the harbour. This caused consternation on our ship because it did not carry a staff large enough to deal with the large amount of signal traffic that this would entail; with the result that some comedian came up to me and said, 'Did you put in for a draft chit to a destroyer?'

When I said yes, he said, 'Well, you've got a draft chit but not to a destroyer. You're going on the ammo ship.'

So off I went to read pages and pages of signals about high-explosive, semi-armour-piercing, and anti-aircraft, pom-pom and every other kind of shell there was.

The much maligned Neville Chamberlain then went off to see Hitler and returned bearing the historic piece of paper and babbling about peace in our time, so the whole process of ammunitioning ships had to be reversed. It goes without saying that there was many a harsh word spoken as a result.

Christmas came and went once more, and it would soon be time for the spring manoeuvres. Rumour had it that that time we would visit San Remo on completion and so we all started saving up in order to make the most of it. In due course we set off once more for Gibraltar. It wasn't a bad place for a run ashore, although with the crews of two fleets on land, the bars did get a bit crowded.

There was one incident during the spring manoeuvres that did brighten up the proceedings somewhat. We were informed that we were to be subjected to a gas attack and therefore had to go and dig out our gas masks. Luckily we had a calm day, and a destroyer approached, dropping canisters in the sea, which started to emit clouds of tear gas. The gas alarm was sounded and we all donned our gas masks. After a minute or two, two overall-clad stokers came through a hatchway and stood leaning over a guard rail, chatting away. A chief spotted them and came rushing up, shouting, 'There's a gas attack on! Why aren't you wearing your gas masks?'

One of them replied, 'I can't make out what you're saying Chief – you'll have to take your gas mask off.'

The chief then repeated himself and the stoker replied, 'I can't smell anything – I've smelt more gas from a stale fart!'

So much for gas attacks at sea.

At last it was finished, and we all returned to Gibraltar prior to dispersing to our designated resorts to sample the goodies. The buzz was confirmed and we were bound for San Remo. Then the blow fell: 'Signalman Kent, report to the ship's office!'

On arrival I was informed that my draft chit had come through and I was to have my bag and hammock packed to be aboard the *Imogen* in two hours. I said goodbye to all my friends and departed after serving on the *Warspite* for nearly two years, man and boy.

4
HMS Imogen

The *Imogen* was launched on 2 June 1937. Displacement 1,350 tons. Crew about 145 officers and men. Speed 36 knots. Cost about £3 million to build. She had four 4.7-inch guns, ten torpedo tubes, odd bits of anti-aircraft weaponry, and large amounts of depth charges mounted aft.

The date was 11 March 1939 when I stepped aboard my first destroyer. This was the life! Goodbye to the spit and polish and the strict discipline of a flagship, and best of all goodbye to watered-down rum. Rum in destroyers was issued neat. The watering-down dated back to the time of Admiral Vernon, nicknamed 'Old Grogg', who decreed that Pusser's rum was too strong and should therefore be diluted with two parts of water. This was made a regulation and therefore it was carried out in all naval barracks and big ships. Destroyers and submarines, however, were allowed to issue neat rum as a sort of perk for the lack of amenities they suffered as compared with big ships. The *Imogen* was in the third destroyer flotilla, which was moored two abreast alongside the mole at Gibraltar.

I shall always remember my first watch. Naturally, with only a staff of four signalmen to share a twenty-four-hour watch system, there could only be one on at a time, and with two boats tied up alongside each other one signalman used to look out for both boats to make life a little easier. I was doing one of the dog watches when the shore base started calling all ships and indicating that a long signal was to follow. I panicked and nipped down to the mess deck to see if someone would write down for me. I was politely told that I would have to write down for myself.

'I've never done it before,' I said.

'Well, now's your chance to learn,' came the reply.

The signal in question was a weather report and shipping

forecast and I stood there reading the Morse. I had no trouble with that, but all the time I was wondering how my writing was going to turn out. Would I be able to read it? The signal finally finished and I looked at my efforts. I could hardly believe my eyes. It was an absolute shambles. Some lines went uphill, some downhill and nearly all running in to each other. It was nearly unreadable. It took nearly half an hour to sort it out and that was done partly by using some imagination and partly looking at the previous day's forecast. No one seemed to notice and it agreed with the forecast I heard on the radio some time later. By experience I found that the secret was to leave about a two-inch gap between each line, so if the lines ran off centre there would be plenty of leeway. It possibly used a lot more paper than necessary but what did it matter? It was only Pusser's signal pad anyway.

One of the first questions I asked on boarding the ship was, 'Where are we off to…? Nice…? San Remo? Or somewhere else just as exotic?'

Back came the reply, 'No, we bloody aren't! It's back to Malta for us. You're not aboard the flagship now.' So it looked as though my hard-earned savings would be dissipated down the Gut.

As I was the junior signalman, I soon made friends with the junior telegraphist, Wally Hammond. His Christian names were actually Charles William Frederick, but matelots never used a proper Christian name if a suitable nickname could be applied. He commiserated with me on the loss of the San Remo visit but promised me that the bars and cabarets of Sliema had a lot to offer and I would enjoy myself just as much – and what's more, it would not be as expensive.

We duly arrived back in Malta, and as promised Wally took me ashore. The *dghaisa* landed us in front of Tony's cocktail bar. Up on the wall behind the bar was a long list of cocktails that Tony said he could dispense for us, and if we could work our way down to the bottom of the list and still be on our feet, we could have free drinks the following night. Of course, this was a challenge that could not be refused. After all, the drinks were only sixpence a go and I was loaded. I can remember starting off in fine style but unfortunately can't remember how we finished. The next night we returned and tried to claim our free drinks, but Tony assured us that we only got about halfway down the list before we staggered away. He did, however, say that if we would like to have another go we could have the first drink on the house, so off we went again… This attempt was similarly unnecessary.

The following night we went to the Cairo bar and cabaret, where Wally rather fancied one of the dancers/sherry girls. Her name was Elizabeth and she was supposed to be a deposed Russian princess, but as about half the cabaret girls also made this claim it was taken with a pinch of salt. She didn't arrive on the scene until fairly late in the evening, by which time Wally and I had shifted quite a few Blue Labels and were fairly merry. She didn't like this, and tried to get Wally to imbibe less, but he gave the impression that I'd led him on and it was all my fault.

Then one night while doing her act, she danced right in front of us then bent right over backwards in what I think is called the 'Crab'. I couldn't resist the temptation and poured a drop of whisky into her navel. The effect was electrifying. She let out a scream and sort of levitated, then grabbed hold of a table knife and chased me out of the bar. As a result I was persona non grata for a few nights, but as she virtually spoke no English and was fluent in German and I had studied German at school, my services as an interpreter were required and I was soon reinstated, following the requisite apology.

It would have been nice to have spent all the time in Malta but there were still exercises and fleet manoeuvres to be carried out at fairly regular intervals. On reflection, these were all a very great waste of time and effort. None of these manoeuvres or deployments were ever put into actual practice during the war. Admittedly, there was the odd anti-aircraft practice. This involved shooting at a canvas drogue towed by a Walrus or Swordfish at about ninety miles per hour, which bore absolutely no resemblance to the air attacks against which we had to try and defend ourselves later on. Similarly, there was no way that depth-charge practice could be carried out in order to be more accurate when the real thing came along. These two procedures seemed to be our two main activities when in later years we did meet the enemy. Still, I suppose Their Lordships had to find some way of keeping the fleet active, and that seemed to be all they could come up with.

There were also visits to places with varying degrees of interest. There were times spent in remote bays somewhere in Greece, in which the accusations of duck shooting were once more levelled at the top brass. However, we did get to places like Split, Dubrovnik and Beirut, which was much more pleasant and peaceful than it is in the present day. I seem to recollect visiting Famagusta in Cyprus and Casablanca, but I can't remember whether on the *Warspite* or *Imogen*. However, I can state categorically that visiting these places with a bunch of matelots and then revisiting them with your wife and family are two completely different experiences.

As it says in the Bible, it came to pass that a messenger had a signal for the Captain. The Captain's cabin door was open so he knocked and stepped across the threshold, only to find the cabin empty. He poked his head through the door of the sleeping cabin to see if he was in there and as he did so he broke wind, lifted up his leg and shook it as though wishing to shake the offending by-product out of his trousers. Unfortunately, the Captain returned just in time to witness this performance.

'You filthy swine!' he shouted. 'Go and put yourself in the first lieutenant's report.'

The messenger then made his way down to the cox'n (who is responsible for discipline on small ships) and told him what he had done.

'You stupid bastard!' said the cox'n, 'What the hell am I going to put on the charge sheet?'

'Don't know, Cox,' was the reply.

'Of course you don't know, neither do I,' said the cox'n. 'You'd better shove off and let me think about it.'

The next morning at the appropriate time, request men and defaulters fell in on the upper deck. The first defaulter was called to the table. He came at the double, and in an endeavour to come to attention in a smart manner and remove his cap, his feet slipped from under him and he shot right under the table. Jimmy (the first lieutenant) had to leap for his life to avoid what resembled a flying tackle, while from underneath the table came an agonised imprecation of 'Jesus Christ!'

It took quite an enormous amount of will to try and keep a

straight face while this lot was sorted out, and in the end the offender was duly given his reprimand and limped away. The next offender was summoned and the cox'n read out the charge.

'Did make a rude noise in an officer's cabin and did emphasise the fact by the shaking of his leg.'

This was too much for one of the attending officers, who let out a huge guffaw, and the proceedings became a bit of a shambles. Eventually the offender was sentenced to three days' stoppage of leave, but as we were sailing the next day it didn't really matter.

At last the day arrived for which we had been waiting. It was time to return to England. Little did we realise that this was the last time we would see Malta at its best. Nearly all the population was employed in looking after the needs of the services, the bars and cafés alive with people and music, the island throbbing with life, and it was very sad to return many years later to find it subdued and quiet, trying to maintain life entertaining tourists. And so in late July we left the island and arrived in Chatham on 1 August 1939.

We packed our bags and hammocks, said a fond farewell to the ship and were transported back to RN barracks. After doing our joining routine and obtaining the requisite card, we departed on two weeks' foreign service leave. There were doubts in our minds as to how long the leave would last, owing to the rather serious events boiling up on the continent due to the machinations of Hitler. Sure enough, within a few days we all received our recall telegram. I remember I had been out for the afternoon, and on arriving home my mother told me of the telegram. She said, 'I've packed all your gear and there is some tea ready, and if you hurry you can catch the 6.30 p.m. train.'

She was rather alarmed when I said, 'You must be joking! Ten o'clock in the morning will be quite soon enough. They won't start the war without me.'

So it was back to barracks to do the leaving routine, which is, in effect, the joining routine in reverse and then back aboard the dear old *Imogen* once more. This was 21 August, and by early September we found ourselves back in Malta once more and we were there when war was declared. Why we were sent out there we never knew. We went back to Gibraltar and started doing anti-submarine patrols in the Straits of Gibraltar. Some bright boy in the Admiralty must have thought U-boats might want to enter the Mediterranean which was ridiculous. There were plenty of rich pickings nearer home. After a few wasted days, there were reports of U-boats in the Bay of Biscay, so we were sent to investigate and, after chasing one or two other sightings, managed to work our way back into home waters and finished up back in Plymouth.

It soon became obvious that destroyers were the maids of all work, as the saying goes. We were continually at sea doing every odd job that came along: U-boat hunting, distress calls, convoy escorts, big ship screening, you name it, we did it.

13 October was a date that I shall always remember. We were out in the Atlantic and received a distress call from a ship that had been torpedoed. Being in the vicinity, we raced to the spot just as she was going down. After sweeping the area to make sure that the U-boat wasn't still lurking, we picked up the survivors and set off back to harbour. Within two hours we picked up a submarine on the Asdics and carried out a depth charge attack. After about the sixth pattern of charges he surfaced, and one of our sharpshooters immediately put a shell through his conning tower. The crew came pouring out of the hatches with their arms held aloft in surrender and within minutes the boat sank, leaving them floundering in the water. Once more we picked up survivors and set off back to Plymouth. If this had been one of those patriotic war films, there would have been crowds cheering us as we arrived back alongside, but in actual fact there were about two dockyard workers to take our mooring lines. Then, after landing our survivors, we were immediately informed that we were duty destroyer and to keep steam at two hours' notice.

Time spent in harbour was very brief, sometimes only long enough to refuel and restock with depth charges and victuals. It was on one of these restocking runs that one of the crew, Tankie (the Butcher), managed to acquire a duffel coat, which was regarded at the time as a bit of a novelty, as this was the first time they had been introduced. The following day, Jimmy, who had been ashore, also arrived on board with a similar garment just

H. M. S. Ganges Shotley Gate Harwich

R.—162. (Revised ~~October,~~ 1916.)

ROYAL ~~MARINES~~ *Navy*.—PASS FOR RECRUITS.

Boy
~~Recruit~~............ *Kenneth Kent*

Royal ~~Marines~~ *Navy*, proceeding by........ *9.45 A.M. Train*

from........ **MANCHESTER**........ to........ *Harwich*

has received his ticket by the........ *L. M. & S. Rly*

DESCRIPTION :—Age (about)........ *15·3* Height.... *5* ....ft.... *7½* ..in.

Hair. *Dark* ... Complexion. *Sallow*

Eyes. *Brown* Dress.... *Brown suit & Tie. no cap.*

The Recruit has in Charge........

and has been subsisted by me to the........ *20ᵗʰ* ..day of.... *November*

19 *35*., inclusive.

Date *20ᵗʰ Nov* 19 *35*

(Actual day of starting.)

.... *Recruiting St........* LT. CR. R.M.

It is requested that the Bearer of this Pass, should he by accident miss his passage, may receive assistance, to forward him to his destination, from all Police Authorities, Railway Officials, and officers of Steamers.

The description given above should be referred to, to prevent an improper use being made of this pass.

Any Report of Irregularity can be addressed to the
Adjutant-General, Royal Marines,
Admiralty, S.W.1.

MEMO.—This Pass must be given to each Recruit as soon as he takes his seat in the train, or embarks, with instructions to be careful to deliver it, on arrival at his destination, to the Sergeant who meets him.

Sta. 166/07.   Sta. 523/16.
R.M. 4156/16..   R.M. 24243/16.
Sta. 117/16.   [2025] 12843/D414 7500 (2) 10/26 3556 G & S 124

Final recruitment for boys in the north of England was done in Deansgate, Manchester, where the boys all foregathered for onward transmission to Shotley. These passes were issued by the recruiting chief together with train tickets and explicit instructions on how to get there.

The author at the start of his naval service.

Aerial view of HMS Ganges, *Shotley.*

Shotley: flag-hoisting competition (author in stripes).

242 Class in Shotley, displaying sheild won in above competition.

Obstacle Cutter Races, HMS Ganges, *1936.*

The mast at HMS Ganges, *manned by the ship's company.*

HMS Warspite, *fleet flagship of the Mediterranean fleet, entering Grand Harbour, Malta, 1938. The ill-fated* Hood *is seen following on.*

HMS Warspite *lying in her berth in Grand Harbour, Malta. The ship lying on the quarter with two funnels is the Italian* Conte-di-Cavour *battleship.*

Bringing the troops back from Crete to Alexandria.

HMS Warspite *during action in the Mediterranean.*

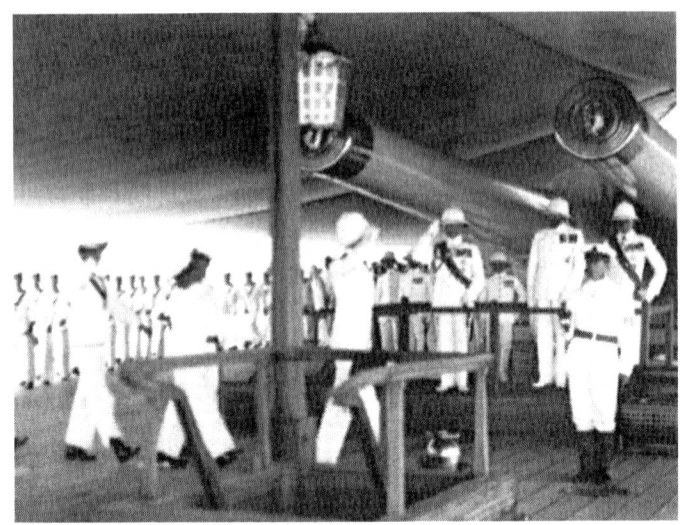

March past the King of Greece on HMS Warspite. *Admiral Sir Dudley Pound (later First Sea Lord) and Captain V C Crutchley are in attendance.*

HMS Barham, *Alexandria, 1938.*

The sad end of HMS Barham, *sunk by an Italian torpedo.*

Captain Guy Grantham, HMS Phoebe.
He was to become Governor of Malta.

The author on HMS Phoebe.

HMS Phoebe.

Neptune *straddled by a stick of bombs, taken from* Phoebe.

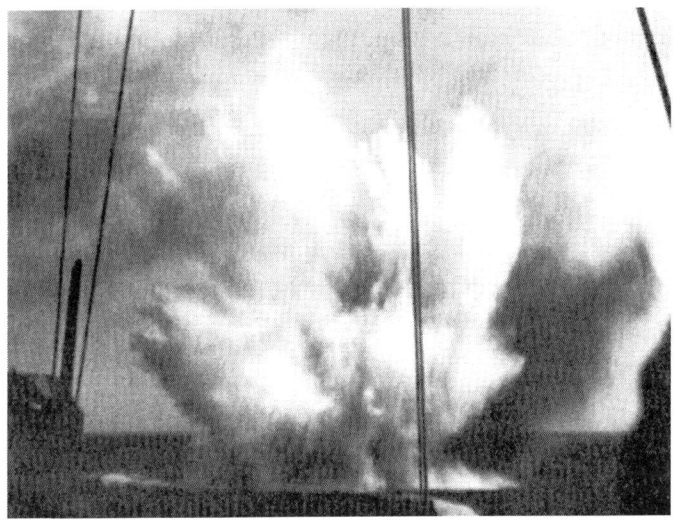

A near miss on HMS Phoebe *from Stukas.*

Malaya *receiving an unwanted gift from high-level bombers.*

The author on the flag deck of HMS Phoebe.

Freetown, 1940.

The author at the end of service.

before we sailed. A couple of nights later as dusk was falling, Tankie was on his way up to the bridge with the auxiliary steaming lights. These are large red and green paraffin lamps for use in case the electric lamps fail. He was wearing his new duffel coat. As he reached the flag deck, Jimmy came round the corner and said, 'Tankie, I've forgotten my cigarettes. Nip down to my cabin, will you?'

Tankie replied, 'I'm just taking the steaming lights up on the bridge,' to which Jimmy said, 'You go and get the fags and I'll take the lamps up.'

Off went Tankie, and Jimmy started to ascend the ladder on to the bridge when Tankie's mate came round the corner saw a duffel-coated figure and shouted, 'Now I've got you where I want you, you old bastard!' Then he rammed his finger up Jimmy's backside.

Jimmy, the first lieutenant, let out an indignant roar and Stripey realised his grievous mistake and vanished. So did every one else. Jimmy came rushing down off the bridge, but the only person to be seen was the quartermaster on the wheel in the wheelhouse, who swore he saw and heard nothing as he was concentrating on steering the ship. Fortunately, Jimmy was a decent sort of bloke and probably realised how the unfortunate mistake had been made and took no action.

In April 1940 we went up to Kyle of Lochalsh to rendezvous with a mass of ships including minelayers. There was a buzz going round that we were going to lay mines in the path of a German Fleet en route to Norway. Unfortunately we were too late. The German Fleet had already passed by and the invasion of Norway had started. We soon became totally involved in the battle for Norway, escorting troopships, hunting U-boats, and avoiding enemy bombers. I well remember hearing about my old ship *Warspite* sailing up one of the fiords and blasting a few Nazi destroyers out of the water. The travel brochures of the present day offer cruises up the Norwegian fiords for a few hundred pounds. We got one for nothing, only ours had a significant difference. We were ferreting out Nazi warships, not a very alluring prospect. Their destroyers were more heavily armed than we were, with 5.9-inch guns as opposed to our 4.7-inch.

Fortunately we drew a blank. The only enemy we encountered was a German trawler. We didn't bother to sink it but we were on a diet of fresh fish for days afterwards.

It wasn't very long before the time arrived for us to evacuate the troops who were being overrun by the 'Nazi hordes' (as Churchill used to call them). It seemed to us as though this would be inevitable from the very beginning. Little do these politicians realise the huge loss of life, money, arms and equipment these token gestures cause. No one in their right mind could ever have expected that the few hundred troops plus the remainder of the Norwegian army could drive out a huge fighting machine like the German Wehrmacht.

Within a few weeks it was all over and we found ourselves in Scapa Flow. Strategically speaking it was an ideal place. For a matelot's run ashore, it was the bottom of the list. In order to try and alleviate the boredom, the REMEs had built a fleet canteen and a large theatre/cinema which put on shows featuring some of the big names in show business who, if they had not joined one of the forces, had become members of ENSA. We saw some fairly good shows but also got our fair share of rubbish.

In July of that year it was reported that the German Fleet had left harbour, so a force of cruisers and destroyers were ordered to put to sea and join battle. We ploughed across the North Sea until we were within range of the Luftwaffe, then the German ships returned to harbour and left us to the tender mercy of the enemy bombers. Fortunately on this occasion they were unsuccessful, and we turned around and set off back to Scapa.

It was well after midnight, and everyone except the watch keepers was asleep, when we were all awakened by the loud crying of the ship's cat. Suddenly there was a tremendous crash and everybody was thrown to the deck as the ship suddenly stopped dead. We all rushed out of the mess and for some reason I climbed up on to the bridge, no doubt to get a better view of what had happened. I walked on to the flag deck and a voice shouted, 'Over here, mate!'

As I looked toward the sound of the voice, I saw the bows of the cruiser *Glasgow* stuck into the side of the bridge. I walked across and climbed aboard with the aid of a couple of helping hands. Within moments of my doing this, flames started rising up from the very place from where I had just climbed. The oil tanks had been punctured and the galley fire had been knocked over and ignited the oil. Lines were thrown across and some of the crew went hand over hand across. A boat was lowered for those who had jumped overboard, and it was a very traumatic sight seeing my mates trying to save themselves.

I was soon ushered down below and could not help wondering what had happened to the little cat. We should all be grateful to her. To be woken by a loud crash or an explosion often causes panic but we were all alert and managed to keep cool, although we didn't hang about. It has been said that animals possess a sixth sense which enables them to foretell disaster, and this proved to be the case. We all hoped the she managed to survive and possibly become a member of the *Glasgow* ship's company. We were all very sad to lose our ship. She had been a happy ship and we had many fond memories on which to dwell. Sadly, one officer and ten ratings were injured and seventeen were killed, among whom were our yeoman of signals and Dickie Beck, our leading signalman.

In the morning we learned that the fleet had been carrying out an alteration of course in thick fog, and a wrong helm order was given owing to a signal being incorrectly interpreted. We also learned that it happened in nearly the same position that Lord Kitchener lost his life by drowning in the *Hampshire*. On arrival back at Scapa we were put on board the *Dunluce Castle*, a clapped-out old merchant ship that acted as stores and depot ship for the fleet. Their stock of stores was not adequate enough to provide over a hundred officers and men with new kit, so we were all supplied with a duffel coat.

At 1600 we boarded the *St Ninian* for passage across to Scrabster on the mainland, and at 2000 we boarded the train for King's Cross. We arrived in London at 1600 the following day, such was the rate of progress during the war. Some two hours later saw us arriving in Chatham Barracks, just in time to be greeted with the banshee wail of the air-raid sirens and were immediately shepherded down a long tunnel to sit on hard benches. Welcome to Chatham!

The next day was spent doing the inevitable joining routine plus the acquisition of new kit. Then came the best thing of all: two weeks survivors' leave. I felt a bit guilty about saying my escapade earned me 'survivors' leave' as I hadn't even got my feet wet, but I was informed that the trauma of this experience made up for it.

Destroyer Lost in Collision

The Admiralty issued the following communiqué last night:

> The Secretary of the Admiralty regrets to announce the loss of H.M. destroyer *Imogen* (Commander C.L. Firth, M.V.O., R.N.) as a result of a collision in dense fog.
>
> One officer and ten ratings were injured, of whom one rating has since died. In addition, 17 ratings are missing, and it is feared that they have lost their lives. The next-of-kin have been informed.

HMS *Imogen* (1,350 tons) was launched in October, 1936, and was one of eight vessels of the Intrepid class ordered under the 1935 naval programme. She had 4.7-inch guns and smaller machine-guns.

HMS IMOGEN

OFFICER:

Injured – Temp. Surgeon-Lieutenant J.W. Ashley, R.N.V.R.

RATINGS:

Died of Injuries – Bradshaw, John W., C.P.O.; Fuller, W.C., Yeo. Sigs.

Missing, Presumed Dead – Aisthorpe, John J., A.B.; Bartlett, Wallace O.F., stoker P.O.; Beck, Richard, leading sig.; Bennett, Wilfred L., ord. art.; Black, Harold F., supply P.O.; Dunk, Albert R.A., stoker P.O.; Fitzpatrick, William, stoker.

Foster, John R., supply asst.; Heasman, Charles, stoker P.O.; Hogben, John H.T., stoker; Lawson, Robert F., ldg seaman; Lifton, Edward S., stoker; Lightening, Arthur E., stoker P.O.; Pittman, Arthur H.S., P.O.; Scott, John H., stoker; Stanyon, Gordon T., A.B.; Turner, Richard, L.S.

Injured – Chalcraft, A., stoker P.O.; Colby, V., P.O.; Luckhurst, R., stoker 1st class; Marshall, S., stoker P.O.; Peters, B., A.B., R.N.V.R.; Reason, S., A.B.; Smith, F., ldg seaman; Trower, V., stoker.

5

HMS Phoebe

Launched on March 1939, she had eight 5.25-inch guns plus
pom-poms, oerlikons and Bofors guns (all anti-aircraft). Displacement 5,450 tons. Complement, 550 men; speed, 33 knots.

I joined the ship on 9 November 1940. For reasons known only
to themselves, the dockyard workers of Govan who built the
ship must have had very little faith in their workmanship.
Comments like, 'She's been thrown together,' and, 'I wouldn't
sail down the Clyde in her,' didn't inspire us with much confidence or fire our enthusiasm. However, despite their gloom, she
passed all her trials without a hitch and was accepted into the
bosom of the Royal Navy.

It was on this ship that I met the best mate I ever had in the
service. His name was Vic Chanter and we seemed to have an
affinity for the same things as regards music, namely the big
American bands and jazz stars. We always seemed to finish our
runs ashore in Glasgow at a dance hall, because at that time the
pubs used to close at 9 p.m. in Scotland, a most disgraceful state
of affairs. We made friends with a young lady who worked behind
the soft drinks counter in one of these dance halls and used to slip
her half a bottle of whisky; then, when we ordered a soft drink
she used to lace it with a liberal amount of whisky from the bottle.
In return for this service she was allowed to take the odd swig
herself. I think her name was Jean, but there again every Scots girl
seemed to be called Jean!

One day we were detailed off to go and decorate the town hall
with signal flags, as the local Royal Naval Association were
holding a dinner and dance in the ship's honour. We had finished
draping the flags and pendants round the wall and were just going
to retire for a pint when some female official in charge of
proceedings told us that the flags didn't look very decorative, and
could we tie some fancy bows on the bottom ends of the

pendants. We had a half-hearted attempt to accede to her wishes, but trying to tie fancy bows in Pusser's bunting is an impossible task so we asked the lady to show us what she wanted. However, after spending a fruitless few minutes trying to show us, she gave it up as a bad job. Then the old music hall artist Leslie Henson arrived and decided that the piano was not in the right position. He asked us to move it round a bit and by the time we finished with him the piano had achieved a full 360-degree turn and was back in the original position!

As a reward for our labours we were invited to the 'do', but realising that this was an officers-only job, we decided that this invitation was rather hollow, and two matelots would not be a welcome sight among the bigwigs of the local council and our ship's officers, so we gave it a miss.

We quite enjoyed our stay in the dockyard but all good things must come to an end and the time arrived for us to put to sea and get on with the war. We had just completed our working-up period, which consists of testing every bit of apparatus and performing endless drills so that we could be regarded as being highly proficient in the use of our equipment, when we received a signal reporting that a German pocket battleship had broken out and put to sea. This caused a panic at the Admiralty, and everything that could float and fire a gun was ordered to sail… a seek-and-destroy job.

I can still remember ploughing through the North Atlantic with a north-westerly gale blowing and the Captain's offer of a pound note for the first man to spot the enemy ship. Luckily she didn't come our way. I spoke to some of the lookouts later on, and to a man they said he could stuff his pound. If they had seen a pocket battleship, they were keeping mum. Who wants to tangle with twelve-inch guns when we only had 5.25s? The Captain was a very courageous man and would have got stuck in – and in all probability blown out of the water. The lads were more practical. They wanted to see out the end of the war, not feed the fish.

After a long and thankfully fruitless search, our fuel ran low and we returned to Greenock. The mail came aboard, and with it, the notification that I was to be rated Leading Signalman if recommended. This was quite unprecedented. To be made a leading hand before receiving the first good-conduct badge (awarded at the age of twenty-one) was unheard of. There was quite a bit of muttering from the old hands about how many years they had had to wait, sometimes into their late twenties before they could pick up the rate. A few remarks like, 'No badge killicks – what's the Navy coming to?' were heard. I couldn't care less what was said. I had worked for it for five years and blessed my good fortune. At the appropriate time, I went before the Captain to be officially rated leading signalman and received his congratulations. He also shared my pleasure, because on his ship he had probably the youngest leading hand in the Navy. He was a great captain, absolutely fearless and a gentleman to his fingertips. He was never heard to raise his voice in anger and was loved by the whole of the ship's company. Some years later when I visited Malta, on looking at the list of governors of Malta I saw his name, Sir Guy Grantham, among the other illustrious figures. A truly great man.

Our next job was to escort a large convoy of ships to Alexandria via the Cape and through Suez, which meant a spell of at least three weeks at sea: not a very enviable prospect. We had to take a diversionary course by sailing quite a long way out into the Atlantic before turning south to avoid enemy aircraft and U-boats. We had been at sea about a week and I had the forenoon watch on the bridge, and as there was nothing happening I decided to clean my telescope. I called down to the flag deck and told them to let me know if any flag hoists went up as I was taking my scope to pieces to clean it. I had just got it taken apart when a shout came up the voice pipe. 'Signal flying L130!'

In the naval code, I knew this meant, 'Suspicious vessel bearing 130,' so I sung out, 'Suspicious vessel bearing 130,' whereupon the officer of the watch immediately sounded the alarms and brought the ship to action stations.

The buzzer sounded from the flag deck voice pipe and a voice said, 'What's all the panic?'

'That signal you just passed up, L130 re suspicious vessel,' I replied.

'It was in the international code, not naval,' came his reply, and this meant alter course to 130 °.

With some apprehension, I had then to explain to the Captain (who had rushed up onto the bridge) how I came to make this blunder, and to my surprise he then asked the officer of the watch how long it had taken the ship's company to close up action stations. On being told they had achieved it in record time, he just suggested that I clean my telescope at a more appropriate time. Like I said, he was a great man.

After what seemed ages, we finally arrived at Freetown. We all thought, What a dump! We went for a run ashore and couldn't find any decent pubs, and the beer was awful. The only incident worthy of note was all the women on the outskirts of town were topless, so one of the lads asked if he could take a photograph (in those days, you only had those box cameras where you peered through a hole in the top). The lady in question agreed, but as he was shaping up she covered her bosom so then negotiations broke out to try to persuade her to remove her hands. She finally agreed on being paid the princely sum of sixpence, to lower her hands so the lads had a whip-round and the snap was duly taken.

After a couple of days stay for refuelling and so on, we set sail, our next port of call being Durban in South Africa. The only incidents of note that occurred to relieve the boredom were firstly, the Crossing the Line ceremonies, and secondly another alarm. The lookouts reported a battleship fighting top in sight to starboard. The Captain immediately ordered action stations and altered course towards the ship in question and rang down for full speed ahead. Had this been a Hollywood movie, the crew would all have been cheering and shouting patriotic slogans. In real life all you hear is phrases like, 'Here we go again,' or 'I hope you can bloody swim!'

Fortunately it turned out to be the *Ramillies*, who had been sent as additional escort as the *Graf Spee* was knocking about in our area, or so it was thought at the time. Once more this demonstrated the courage of Guy Grantham, who would have fought to the death in an effort to save the convoy.

We finally arrived at Durban after what seemed ages at sea. We found Durban to be the friendliest port we had ever visited. Our arrival alongside was greeted by a lady on the town hall balcony singing 'Land of Hope and Glory' through a huge amplifier, and in later years she was featured on a worldwide newsreel. People were waiting in their cars to give us a lift into town, and innumerable invitations were given out for us to visit them in their homes. Public transport was free to servicemen, and beer was sixpence a pint. Likewise, a tot of brandy was only sixpence, but it was Cape brandy and pretty powerful stuff. Durban was a place I shall always remember, and regrettably our stay was all too short.

We were now sailing in the Indian Ocean and used to spend quite some time watching the flying fish, trying to figure out if they really flew, or was it just the impetus as they came out of the water? There was no U-boat activity in this part of the world, which meant that we could take a more direct route up the east coast of Africa, and so it didn't seem too long before we reached Port Suez. This was not much of a place for a run ashore. The only point of interest was the entertainment provided by very tiny children known as *gilli-gilli* boys. They would approach your table while you were having a drink and give demonstrations of sleight of hand. They could pluck eggs and similar objects out of the air, and there was even one who could produce live chicks from nowhere. We only stopped long enough to pick up a pilot, then off we went through the canal, finally arriving in Alexandria. We made it without losing a single ship.

Up to now, things had been pretty quiet in the Mediterranean, apart from the Battle of Cape Matapan, but Mussolini began flexing his muscles. He began to realise that he was, more or less, the sleeping partner of the Axis powers and decided to do something to impress his friend Hitler. He considered a nation of about 7 million people to be easy pickings against his 45 million, so Greece became the target for his evil intentions. He had an army of 150,000 troops in Albania and estimated that the Greeks could only muster about 75,000, so he denounced Greece for her non-neutral attitude and demanded the occupation of strategic positions in Greece. Before Greece could reply to these unreasonable demands, he invaded in true fascist style. Unfortunately, his timing was severely at fault, as the rainy season in November was not the best of times to go pushing through the Balkan Mountains. Spurred on by a spirit of patriotism and indignation, the Greeks fought back with such force and determination that by the end of December a quarter of Albania was in Greek hands, as well as 5,000 prisoners.

Hitler was far from pleased to learn that such a small nation could show such defiance to the mighty all-conquering Axis powers and decided that it was time to take charge of affairs. He sent his Twelfth Army, which attacked the Greeks through Yugoslavia. This stirred up the 'brains' in Whitehall. Churchill was well known for his affinity with the Balkans and it was not long before orders were received to land a British force in Greece. Here we go again…

Within days the poor old squaddies were boarding various types of ships for passage to Greece. Forgotten were the memories of the Norwegian landings and the futility of that operation, and apart from anything else, the Greeks did not *want* British troops landed, but they were persuaded by Anthony Eden. Some people blamed Churchill; others said he left it to Wavell to decide. Who knows? All we knew was that we were taking troops to Greece, and in a few weeks we would be bringing out the lucky ones who survived the conflict.

Ours was a motley collection of ships. There were cruise liners converted to troop carriers, coastal steamers and tramp steamers escorted by various cruisers and destroyers, *Phoebe* included. It wasn't long before enemy reconnaissance planes spotted the convoy heading for the Greek mainland, and as soon as we came into range, the Luftwaffe and Italian Air Force were waiting to give us an unwanted welcome. The Italians' lack of enthusiasm for danger was amply demonstrated by the nature of their torpedo bomber attacks, which were delivered far out of range of our anti-aircraft fire. This meant that we had plenty of time to take the necessary evasive action to avoid their torpedoes. Their bomber pilots had a similar dislike of gunfire and used to bomb from about 20,000 feet. Not so the German Stuka pilots, with their dive-bombers. They came in so close that it sometimes seemed as if they were going to dive down our funnels!

The speed of a convoy is the speed of the slowest ship, and we had a millstone round our necks in the shape of a rust-ridden old Greek tramp steamer with the name of *Popi*. Naturally it was christened 'Popeye', and during all the air attacks that we sustained, not a single enemy aircraft went anywhere near it. It was worth more afloat as far as they were concerned as it kept us pinned down… or maybe they thought it wasn't worth a bomb and might sink by natural causes anyway.

We finally made it to Greece and landed about 56,000 Allied troops. Poor devils. We felt desperately sorry for them and blessed our luck that we could get away out of it and back to Alexandria.

As anticipated, it was all over by 21 April. The Greek army surrendered. Their troops, using horses and in some cases oxen, were no match for the mighty German Panzer Divisions, plus the fact that the Allied troops were unaccustomed to fighting in mountainous terrain and not equipped to deal with modern tanks and air attacks from Stukas.

So it was a case of 'off to Greece and bring the lads back again'. We did not expect that there would be all that many to bring back, but the brilliance of Sir Henry Maitland Wilson's organisation was responsible for 43,000 troops being extricated from the Nazi clutches. Regrettably, 11,000 were left behind, plus nearly all their equipment and weapons. Of the rescued 43,000, we landed 27,000 men in Crete, as there were expectations of an airborne landing on that island.

Churchill communicated this fact to General Wavell in North Africa, saying that heavy airborne attacks were to be made on Crete and added the bloodthirsty comment that it ought to be a fine opportunity for killing German parachute troops. General Freyburg was appointed to organise the defence of the island and worked hard to bring things to a state of readiness. On 16 May, he reported that with the help of the Navy, Crete could be held against any attack.

On 19 May the Luftwaffe struck, and the three airfields were subject to severe attacks, with the result that the RAF fighters stationed there were withdrawn for their own safety. The next day the invasion began. Many of the first 3,500 were slain but 3,000 more were sent in, being reinforced by troop-carrying gliders. As there were no British aircraft on the scene, they had the freedom of the air, and German troop carriers were pouring in at the rate of twenty an hour.

There seems to be more than one theory about what went

wrong. The main reason was the withdrawal of the troops defending the main airfield, in order to launch a counter-attack on another German-held position. This proved abortive. Other withdrawals were made as German seaborne reinforcements were expected, which said much for their faith in the Navy. Their lack of confidence in our ability to deal with any seaborne forces was totally unfounded. The German foot soldiers were embarked mostly in Greek caiques which were helpless against three British cruisers and four destroyers, which sailed in among them and virtually sank the lot. It was most distressing for us to observe such a senseless loss of life as these defenceless vessels were sent to the bottom and their occupants drowned. It infuriated the German Stuka pilots, who attacked with renewed ferocity. A second convoy was despatched, escorted by a reluctant Italian destroyer and met with the same fate, including the destroyer. During all these actions we were under constant attack from enemy aircraft at great cost to the Navy. The cruisers *Fiji* and *Gloucester* were sunk, plus three destroyers, including Mount-batten's *Kelly*.

It became clear that the battle was being lost, and by 28 May it was decided to evacuate. We succeeded in bringing off about 15,000 troops, although some 13,000 British troops and 5,000 Greeks were left behind. We were far from happy about this, but the Mediterranean Fleet had been decimated and it was impossible to take another man. We had picked everybody off the beach, and those remaining had already been captured or were fighting a rearguard action. The Germans lost about 16,000 men and 170 troop-carrying aircraft, so although they had occupied Crete, the German Seventh Air Division, commanded by General Student, was almost decimated. Our fleet lost three cruisers, six destroyers and twenty-nine small ships, and naval casualties amounted to 2,000 men.

My mate Vic Chanter seemed to have a singular disregard for danger. He was very keen on photography, and during some of our worst air attacks he could be seen out on the flag deck taking action shots. His one ambition at that time was to get a head-on picture of an attacking dive bomber releasing its bomb and I once heard him cursing because the pilot pulled out of his dive before he could get a decent shot. In those days, the cameras were fairly primitive, which made his work all the harder, and credit must be given to him for the pictures he managed to obtain. Alas, when I left the ship I lost track of him, which happens to us all as time goes by.

Hitler, knowing that General Wavell had sent a large part of his army to Greece, strengthened his forces in North Africa and appointed General Erwin Rommel to take charge of affairs, probably the wisest decision he ever made. On 31 March he launched a ferocious attack on Wavell's weakened forces. They were driven back as far as Sollum in Egypt, where the attack lost its momentum. The only part not captured was the port of Tobruk. This was heavily defended by about 23,000 men, of whom 15,000 were Australian. This may have been a thorn in Rommel's side, as it tied up one German division and four Italian divisions. It also meant (on the negative side) that the town had to be maintained with supplies of food ammunition and relief troops. Another job for the Navy.

As can be readily appreciated, General Wavell was not the happiest of men, and his lot became an even more unhappy one when a revolt broke out in Iraq. There was a treaty which permitted our troops on Iraqi soil (or should we say sand?), but on 2 May the Iraqis laid siege to a British cantonment and RAF base at Habbaniya. I mention this because we became involved in what was known to us as the 'Syrian piss-up'. As the flagship of the Admiral commanding the cruiser squadron had been damaged, he brought his staff aboard *Phoebe*, and along with *Neptune* and a few old destroyers we sailed for that area of the Mediterranean to sort out the naval involvement.

With the permission of the French high commissioner, the Germans and Italians had established air bases at Damascus, Rayak and Palmyra in Syria, and it seemed that the port of Beirut was in their hands, too. For reasons known only to themselves, the French forces in this part of the world threw in their lot with the Germans, and so we found ourselves fighting our former allies.

One day, as we were abreast the coast in the vicinity of Beirut, I read a signal from one of the escorting destroyers: 'Enemy in sight bearing 080 degrees.' We went to action stations and as they drew near we identified them as three French destroyers. We turned toward them and opened fire when the guns came into range. They immediately did a sharp about turn and beat a hasty retreat back to harbour, with us in hot pursuit. We didn't seem to be making much headway and suddenly a barrage of high-calibre shells fell about our ears. We were being bombarded by the shore batteries. (Had the three destroyers been decoys? we asked ourselves.)

Our admiral (Rear Admiral King) didn't wait to find out. (You don't argue with shore batteries.) 'Let's get out of this,' he said.

'Hard a-port,' said the Captain, and away we went out of harm's way. The Admiral was a man after our own hearts and didn't do anything daft like trying to swap punches with the shore batteries. Besides which, ours were the only ships left intact after the Crete mauling.

There didn't seem much point in patrolling up and down the Syrian coast. There seemed to be nothing to do except to take a few potshots at any enemy tanks we espied going along the coast road. Due to the efforts of Major General Clark, who relieved Habbaniya on 31 May, and General Wilson, who invaded Syria and Lebanon, and not forgetting the stirring efforts of Glub Pasha and his Arab Legion, the uprising was squashed and an armistice signed on 14 July, giving the Allies the right to occupy Syria. This was shortly followed by the Anglo-Russian occupation of Persia, which enabled Wavell to sleep a little easier in his bed (but not much).

On our return to Alexandria, I was in for a surprise, which I received with mixed feelings. It was in the shape of a draft chit. The reason being that when I was rated up to Leading Signalman, the *Phoebe* then had a spare killick – me – and when the destroyer *Griffin* lost her killick, who had done his stint of foreign service, the fleet drafting office cast around for a spare body and I was put in the frame. Therefore, goodbye *Phoebe*. I wasn't too happy about going. I had a lot of friends who I would probably never see again, and cruisers didn't put in as much sea time as destroyers. Still, that was the luck of the draw, so on 17 August 1941 I joined the *Griffin*.

6
HMS Griffin

Griffin was a 'G'-class destroyer launched in 1935 and commissioned in 1936. She had four 4.7-inch guns, one anti-aircraft gun and six torpedoes in two triple mountings. Her speed was 36 knots and she had a complement of 145 officers and men.

Having packed my bag and hammock, I humped them down into a waiting boat. As these are quite a burden for one man to shoulder, I had to leave my portable gramophone and considerable stock of records behind. This machine was my pride and joy and had cost the princely sum of three pounds. It had to be wound up with a handle, and the steel needles had to be replaced after every ten records or so. I can still hear some of those records today, although the quality has been considerably improved by digital remastering: bands and orchestras led by people like Tommy Dorsey, Artie Shaw and Bennie Goodman. I lived in hope that I would be able to go back on board *Phoebe* to retrieve these treasured possessions at some later date.

The *Griffin* was tied up alongside a jetty when I boarded her. A large horde of Egyptian dockers were loading her with stores and ammunition, which took them the best part of the day. The last thing to be loaded was a long gun barrel, which took about fifty of them to lift and carry, accompanied by incantations, exaltations and similar noises of encouragement which seem to be customary among the races in that part of the world.

Next came a squad of unhappy-looking Australian soldiers, who filed aboard and disappeared down below, and at 1600 we set off for Tobruk. These runs were never without incident. We were always attacked by some form of enemy aircraft, either torpedo bombers or Stukas, but luckily we always managed to remain unscathed. It was always a matter of some surprise to us that when the sea was a little choppy, some of the Aussies down below who were bound for the thick of the fighting in the desert used to say, 'Bugger this for a life! I wouldn't like to have to stop aboard these things all the time' – just because they got a bit seasick. We were only too pleased to dump the cargo and get the hell out.

On arrival at Tobruk, every member of the ships' company, including the officers, helped to unload. It took the Arabs nearly a whole day to load; it took us less than an hour to unload. The gun barrel, which took about fifty Arabs, was grabbed by about ten matelots and slung over the side onto the jetty. I suppose the thought that enemy shells may start to fall about our ears at any minute was some form of encouragement.

One destroyer, the *Havoc*, was the cause of amusement on these runs. Before arriving in Tobruk she always used to make a signal requesting to proceed independently after unloading, as her speed was restricted owing to an engine room defect. I think it was alleged her speed was only 21 knots at best. Her speed of unloading must have been phenomenal because she was always first to leave harbour, and although we could do well over 30 knots on the way back, no one ever caught her, and she was always tied up alongside when we arrived back in harbour.

There were many other jobs to be done besides keeping Tobruk topped up with supplies. One was providing an anti-submarine screen round the big ships on the odd occasions when they put to sea. It was on such a mission that a disaster occurred which I shall never forget. Admiral Cunningham put to sea with the fleet on an offensive sweep and we were steaming along one calm afternoon when we heard a loud detonation. I was on the bridge at the time, and on looking round saw the battleship *Barham* turning out of line and listing very heavily. Suddenly there was a tremendous explosion and she blew up. Within seconds, what had once been a mighty battleship of 35,000 tons became a few pieces of scattered wreckage. Nobody expected anyone to live through such a holocaust and we were amazed, and delighted, to learn eventually that there were over 300 survivors. Later on, the cruiser *Penelope* was torpedoed and sunk just outside Alexandria harbour.

Back in harbour in Alexandria, life was fairly peaceful. We were rarely troubled with air attacks but the *Queen Elizabeth* (the battleship, not the liner) and the *Warspite* became what must have been the first victims of frogmen and limpet mines. During the night there were two muffled explosions, and next morning these two mighty battleships were seen lying on the bottom. Fortunately, the water was not too deep and their upper works were still above the surface. This was the work of the Italians who, after attaching the mines, sat on the mooring buoys waiting for the bang. Naturally they were spotted, dragged on board, and incarcerated for the rest of the war.

During the preceding few months, the Japanese had been steadily advancing westwards, having taken Singapore and most of Burma, and it was therefore considered desirable to have a stronger naval force in that part of the world to defend Kenya and operate in the waters around India and Ceylon.

Therefore a force was established to be based at Mombasa in Kenya, ships being drawn from the Home and Mediterranean Fleet. The battleships *Resolution* and *Prince of Wales* and the battlecruiser *Repulse* and various cruisers came from the Home Fleet and among those drawn from the Mediterranean Fleet was the *Griffin*.

Just before we left harbour, I heard that the *Phoebe* had been hit in the bows with a torpedo, but fortunately no one was hurt. Despite the doleful prognostications and lack of faith in her by her builders, she managed to make it back to harbour. Much to my disgust, I heard that she was to be patched up and then sent off to the Brooklyn Navy Yard. I had always wanted to go to New York and had only just missed it by a matter of days!

After the Mediterranean, the Indian Ocean seemed quite peaceful. There were no blackout regulations in Mombasa, and it was quite pleasant to go to sea without the expectation of a stick of bombs falling about our ears at any moment. During the course of our activities, I can remember calling in at such exotic places as Bombay, Ceylon, Madagascar and the Seychelles without experiencing any unpleasant incidents. It came as a great shock to hear of the sinking by the Japanese of the *Repulse* and the *Prince of Wales*. We had been escorting them only a few days previously.

Although I originally volunteered for service in destroyers, that was in peacetime, which was a different kettle of fish to service in wartime, and I was getting fed up with the constant chasing about done by these boats. As luck would have it, I was chatting to a killick signalman in a bar ashore who was on the *Resolution*, and he said he rather fancied going back to destroyers, so without further ado, I arranged to swap with him. On 26 April 1942 I said goodbye to the *Griffin*.

7

HMS Resolution

Built in 1916, she had eight fifteen-inch guns, twelve six-inch guns, eight four-inch anti-aircraft guns and sundry other anti-aircraft weapons. Displacement, 33,000 tons; length, 580 feet; complement, approximately 1,100 officers and men.

It was quite a relief to be part of a ship's company and know that within a few hours we would not have to put to sea yet again. A nice little quiet spell in harbour was just what the doctor ordered. Admittedly, life on a big ship isn't quite as free and easy as on the boats (destroyers), but lying alongside a quiet and peaceful jetty made up for that. One problem was the heat. Mombasa lies almost on the equator and in the centre of our mess deck was the galley servery, from which the hot meals were dispensed during lunchtime. The heat given out from the servery plus the normal heat of the tropics made things rather uncomfortable. We seemed to be constantly perspiring. Also, so much water was needed that the ship's condensers could not keep up with the demand, and we had water rationing of one gallon a day per man.

On the occasions when we did put to sea, conditions were far superior to those on other ships because, although she may have been an old ship, the compass platform on *Resolution* was completely covered in and sealed off from the elements. No more standing, soaked to the skin, in pouring rain. No more getting drenched by spray coming up over the top. This was the life!

Life got even better on 1 June. As the size of the fleet was increasing, it was decided to establish a signal station on shore to be manned by the Royal Navy and Kenya Navy signal staff to take care of the shore signal traffic, and I was fortunate enough to be one of the chosen few to man this station. This was what every matelot dreams of: a nice cushy shore job. To accommodate the staff, a large area of land was cleared at Kilindini (part of

Mombasa) and a number of long huts were built. These were constructed of wooden frames to which was attached hessian. This was then sprayed with wet cement, leaving a gap of about a foot between the floor and the hessian. This was done to keep the huts cool and permit the air to circulate. Unfortunately, it did not prevent visitations from the odd snake or scorpion or other undesirable creatures peculiar to that part of the world. The roof was made of a kind of thatch.

The camp (or 'shore base' as it was called) was given the title HMS *Tana*, and was under the jurisdiction of the Royal Kenya Navy. This meant that, being white, we were not permitted to do any manual work. Had we been transported to some sort of Shangri-La? we asked ourselves. A large laundry bag was placed at the end of each hut every morning, into which we would place our dirty washing. It was then taken away, washed and ironed and returned the next day. When mealtimes arrived, we wandered across to the dining hall, where our meals were served up to us. Our place of work was a couple of miles away and we were transported to and fro in large American Buick cars driven by a native driver. No piling into the back of a Pusser's lorry in this navy!

The signal station was situated in the compound of the coast 'A' gun battery, which was manned by soldiers from one of the East African regiments. As we arrived at the gate, a fierce-looking African soldier used to leap out and thrust a rifle in our faces and shout, 'Halt! Who goes there?'

Our officer then had to give him a code word which had previously been supplied. One of our officers (a fiery Scot) used to become incensed with this performance and when challenged always used to shout, 'Stop buggering about and open the bloody gate!' But he met with scant success, and still had to say the magic word.

From the tower we could see the activities of the battery, and it soon became obvious that these East Africans took their soldiering very seriously. They never walked or strolled anywhere. They always marched themselves, and if only three or four were going somewhere they would involuntarily form themselves into a rank and one of them would then march them off. All we could hear all day was people going, 'Left right, left right!'

One day there appeared on the noticeboard a notice that a football match had been arranged between a team from the combined East African coast battery and a team from the British Fleet. Both team sheets were published, and it was noted with some anticipation that the fleet team was completely represented by professional footballers who had been called up or were volunteers. Such famous teams as Liverpool, Arsenal and Tottenham were represented.

The day of the match arrived and the ground was full. The town had quite a decent stadium. The teams took the field, and to our amazement we observed that the Africans wore no boots. They were all barefooted. Comments like, 'They don't stand a chance,' and, 'They'll get slaughtered' were bandied around the ground.

This turned out to be quite true but it wasn't the Africans who got slaughtered. It was the matelots! I have seen many football matches in my time but I have never seen such an exhibition of skill, dexterity and ball control. One reason that was given was that the bare feet enabled them to get more feel of the ball. Another, that the matelots were cooped up in ships all day and could not keep as fit as those on shore. Whatever the reason, it was a match I shall long remember.

To add to the joys of living ashore, some benevolently minded person decided that it would greatly assist morale if we could be given a few days' leave away from the environs of service life, so after a few weeks, together with a colleague, I found myself on a list to have a week in Nairobi, Kenya's capital. We were given railway warrants and some cash for lodging allowance, and duly set off for a week of relaxation. On arrival in Nairobi, we called at the information centre to enquire about some likely lodgings and were given the address of an old lady who lived on the outskirts of the city.

She provided us with a comfortable bedroom and she had two black servants who waited on us hand and foot. We were having a game of bowls on the second day when two Kenyans asked us if we could give them a game, to which we agreed. They seemed to enjoy our company and invited us back to their house for a meal.

From that time on we spent quite a lot of time with them, sightseeing during the day, and then in the evening, as guests at their social club which proved to be quite a lively place, with entertainment and dancing. We had a thoroughly enjoyable week and it was with some regret that we made our way back to Mombasa.

Back at the camp, it was not a bed of roses in the ensuing weeks. I caught malaria, followed by yellow jaundice. The treatment was pretty gruesome: no butter or margarine, in fact no fat of any kind, and regular doses of Epsom salts, three times a day. The hospital, as such, was a converted house, and the facilities were pretty inadequate and I was very glad when I was finally discharged, fit for duty. Luckily I was just in time to take an exam for yeoman of signals (equivalent to petty officer), which I managed to pass.

On 29 January 1943, I, along with the other signalmen from the *Resolution*, was recalled to the ship. We were not best pleased and such phrases as 'I thought it was too good to last' sprung to mind, but on arrival back on board we learned, to our delight, that the ship was going down to Durban for a spell in dock.

We set sail a couple of days later, and after a quiet passage through the Indian Ocean we arrived in Durban to the accompaniment of 'Land of Hope and Glory' from the town hall balcony. She was still at it! Things hadn't changed. The people were still marvellous, and we were overjoyed to learn that we would be there for quite a few months.

One of the features of this city is a rather unique type of zoo. It consists entirely of snakes with a large compound in the centre about a quarter the size of a football pitch, surrounded by a smooth four-foot wall. This was the cobra compound, where every type of cobra in the world could be found. Round the sides of the snake park (as it was called) were located glass cages in which reposed mambas, boa constrictors, pythons, rattlesnakes, green tree snakes… you name it, they had it. It seems a strange fact of life that a creature that fills nearly everyone with fear and revulsion should prove such a popular attraction, and I am told, by a recent visitor, that it is still going strong to this day.

In no time at all I had made friends with one of the families, who invited me to their home and made me welcome whenever I wished to visit them, which was quite often. I was just beginning to enjoy life when I was suddenly told to pack my bag and hammock and join the *Gambia* for passage to the UK.

I had been abroad for nearly two and a half years and it was now time to return to my native land. I must admit to rather mixed feelings on this move. Here I was, exchanging the bright lights and the fleshpots of Durban for the dark and murky streets of Chatham and Rochester, plus the little goodies that Adolf cared to send our way, such as buzz bombs and other unfriendly artefacts.

8
HMS Gambia

A cruiser, completed in November 1940. Displacement, 8,000 tons. Complement, 980 officers and men. Length, 550 feet. She had twelve six-inch guns, eight four-inch and sundry other anti-aircraft guns.

I joined this ship on 13 May 1943 and soon became aware that a modern cruiser had a lot more to offer in the way of comfort than an old pre-First World War battleship. She was a very happy ship, but as everyone was on the way home I suppose it was to be expected.

A couple of days after leaving Durban I was doing a watch on the bridge and it was a calm and peaceful afternoon. The calm was broken by the quartermaster's voice from the wheelhouse asking, 'The padre requests permission to take the wheel, sir.'

The officer of the watch then replied, 'Very well, but stay in the vicinity.'

'Aye aye, sir,' replied the QM. 'Padre now on the wheel.'

A few minutes later the navigating officer came on to the bridge and asked the officer of the watch to take a sight for him, or some such request. The officer of the watch duly departed to the back of the bridge while the navigator consulted his notes, then went across to the wheelhouse voicepipe and gave the order, 'Starboard ten.'

It was hilarious to see the look of consternation appear on his face when the ship started turning to port. He nearly rammed his face down the voicepipe and shouted, 'I said *starboard* ten, you bloody idiot! I'll come down there and jam your balls in the wheel and put starboard ten on. Then you'll bloody soon know where it is.'

Just then the officer of the watch returned from the back of the bridge and said, 'Oh. I'm sorry, pilot. I forgot to tell you. The

Padre's on the wheel.' The navigator replied, 'Oh, Christ! Well, steer 020 degrees – I'm off!' Then he vanished down below, to the accompaniment of loud guffaws from the remainder of the bridge personnel.

The padre appeared a few minutes later and remarked, 'Pilot seemed a bit upset.'

As it seemed such an easy-going ship I asked one of the administration staff what the chances were of getting my Yeoman's rate and was told, 'Why not give it a whirl? You've nothing to lose.'

So without more ado, I put in my application. In due course I went before the Captain and he said he saw no reason why I should not be made yeoman, and not only granted my request but backdated it to the date when I passed the exam in January. To add to the delight at my good fortune, we were then informed that our destination was Liverpool. Those of us who had sampled the delights of runs ashore in Liverpool were overjoyed, particularly so in my case, as I had a pocketful of back pay waiting to be suitably diminished.

We finally docked in Bootle, and everyone wanted to get off the ship and back to barracks, followed by two or three weeks' leave. Not me! The thought of returning to the Methodist household, sitting listening to 'ITMA' and 'Workers' Playtime' or reading library books was far from appealing. I became very popular when I volunteered to be the last to leave the ship and I was the recipient of many grateful tots of rum.

The ship's company dwindled until there were only a few of us left, and just as we were finally getting ready to leave (with much reluctance) we were informed that the ship was to be transferred to the New Zealand Navy, and would we mind staying behind for a few weeks to show the new crew the ropes? I was overjoyed. It was a case of 'My cup runneth over', and I would stay as long as was required.

They soon started arriving on board and getting settled in. They were a great set of blokes and I made very many friends, so much so that I was asked if I would stay with the ship and sign on with the New Zealand Navy. It meant that I would have to spend five years in New Zealand, but as I had had my fill of Foreign

Service I declined. They were very persuasive and at least three of them offered me a well-paid job when I had finished my service if I wanted to stop out there. I sometimes wish I had taken up the offer.

All good things must come to an end, and so it was that the *Gambia* was due to sail for New Zealand on 25 October. I was therefore obliged to pack my goods and chattels and bid farewell to the many friends I had made on the ship and ashore. Back to Chatham Barracks I went, because although all communication ratings now lived at Cookham, they still had to do the dreaded joining routine at the main barracks, and then be transported to Cookham. Off I trudged on the rounds of the various departments, and everything was going well until I arrived at the medical section. Here, they had added an eyesight test (probably to give the sickbay tiffies something to do).

The usual ritual was observed, namely, a card over one eye and the instruction to read the bottom line. I was nonplussed. I could hardly see the bottom line, let alone read it, and could only just read the third from the top with only three fairly large letters in it. I was then sent to the medical officer (ophthalmic), who did further tests and pronounced that I would have to wear glasses, and as all members of the signals branch had to have 20–20 vision, I was informed that I could no longer go to sea. It dawned on me that the reason for me being unaware of my failing sight was the fact that when on watch every signalman has a pair of binoculars strung round his neck or a telescope under his arm, and these instruments are used on every suitable opportunity, probably more so in my case. I wasn't too perturbed about never being able to feel a deck beneath my feet again. I had had more than my fair share of sea time!

To become a chief it was necessary to be a confirmed yeoman of signals, and this confirmation had to be achieved by undergoing a six-week intensive course on all forms of communications at the main signal school at Leydene near Petersfield in Hampshire. I kept quiet about the dodgy eyesight, as I didn't wear the spectacles provided, and applied to go on this course and luckily was accepted.

I departed on 29 May 1944, and on arrival in Hampshire I was amazed to see the large volume of military traffic on the roads, including tanks and mobile guns. Then the memorable date, 6 June, arrived and they all vanished. D-Day had arrived, but we just carried on with our academic studies and listened to the radio for the news of the landings. The signal school complex was centred round a large country mansion which was the property of Lady Peal (the former actress Beatrice Lilley), and the huts in which we lived were built in the extensive grounds of the manor. It was a beautiful setting and quite enjoyable, despite the efforts required by ourselves to amass large amounts of new knowledge. On 15 July, the course was over, and we all returned to our respective depots. After settling down at Cookham I went through the necessary request routine and became a confirmed yeoman. There were no more exams to pass and in due course, if I stayed in the service long enough, I would eventually be made a chief yeoman, the highest rank on the lower deck.

For some time I had been having some abdominal pain, and on reporting to the sick quarters was informed that I had a hernia. There are no waiting lists for operations in the Royal Navy, and was told to go and pack enough things in my case to last at least a month and report back to sick quarters within a quarter of an hour. This done, I was immediately transported to Gillingham Royal Navy Hospital, where the operation was carried out the next day. I was then required to spend three weeks in bed. Nowadays, patients have the operation and are up and about within two days. I then had to spend a further three weeks in hospital indulging in the required therapeutic exercises to aid complete recovery. Eventually I was pronounced fit and returned to Cookham, with a chit to inform whomever it may concern that I was on light duty for a period of six months.

Life became rather tedious. I became an instructor and there is nothing worse than trying to instruct people who are not interested and just don't want to know. I wondered if it was possible to get away from Cookham to some other shore base. It happened that I still kept getting draft chits for appointments in ships, but these were quashed when I produced a chit from the medical officer stating that I could not go to sea. Being aware of how the minds of the inhabitants work in the drafting office, I knew it was no good volunteering for a shore base somewhere else, so the next time I got a draft chit for a ship I went into the drafting office, produced my medical exemption chit and then said, 'It's no good you keeping sending me draft chits. I'm quite happy in Cookham Camp, and there's nothing you can do about it.'

As I left the office I heard the words, 'We'll see about that – clever bugger!'

A week or two later I was summoned to the drafting office, where a draft chit was slapped in my hand for the Port War Signal Station at Scapa Flow.

'There you are,' said our friend. 'How do you like that?'

'OK, you win,' I replied, feigning disappointment, and departed with a bogus solemn expression. I couldn't show any signs of pleasure – he might have cancelled it. Scapa was not what I had quite expected, but anything was better than the boring existence at Cookham.

9
Cookham and Scapa

It was with a sense of doubtful anticipation that I packed my bag and hammock on 20 October 1944 and set off on the long journey up to Scapa. By rights I should correctly refer to it as the Orkneys, but in the service it's always referred to as Scapa. In winter this journey is particularly harrowing, owing to the bitter cold one has to endure on reaching the Highlands in Scotland. In peacetime all trains have the locomotives double-headed, but under the exigencies of wartime this was not possible, with the result that when the engine had to tackle the more steep gradients on the track it needed every ounce of steam available to be able to cope with the effort, and therefore there was none available for heating carriages. I have even seen people doubling up and down in the corridor in an effort to get warm. Actually the weather was fairly mild for October, so it wasn't too bad on this occasion.

I arrived at Scrabster the next morning and was transported to Lyness on the island of Hoy on the old ferry, *St Ninian*. Lyness is the shore base of the fleet and seemed to be a hive of activity. As well as the necessary storage depots and living quarters, there was a large services canteen and a spacious cinema/theatre which had been entirely built by the REMEs, or so I was told. My destination, the signal station, was situated on the island of Flotta, which stands at the entrance to Scapa Flow, so the next part of the journey was in a local drifter which had been commandeered by the Navy for the duration of the war.

The pier master on Flotta was an old chief who also had a quite profitable sideline as a sort of provider. Anything you wanted, you saw Chiefie: whisky, duty-free fags, lobsters, crabs, you name it – he could more than likely get it. He greeted me on landing and promptly arranged transport to take me to the other end of the island, where the signal station was located. On arrival

I was quite pleasantly surprised to find a very well laid out camp with very comfortable living quarters. There was a chief and PO's mess and canteen and we all had separate cabins. The other ranks had warm huts and a nice dining hall and canteen as well. The chief and PO's canteen was run on a voluntary basis. There were no opening or closing times as such and the beer was supplied in large eighteen-gallon barrels.

There was no piano in the mess, but I came across an old piano accordion and having a slight keyboard knowledge and an ability to play by ear, I soon worked out how the base chords were arranged and was soon able to knock out some fair tunes. I was practising one afternoon when a lad by the name of Bill Wylie popped his head round the door and said, 'I like the sound of that. I play the piano for the lads in the ratings canteen, so do you fancy bringing the squeezebox down there, and we'll see if we can make some good sounds.'

We seemed to hit it off straight away and after one or two rehearsals we plucked up courage to give our first performance. It proved very popular and when we weren't on watch we gave a show nearly every night. On one occasion there was a party of soldiers visiting from a camp at the other end of the island, and one of them asked us if we would come and play for them one night. They asked what our fee was and our reply was, 'Just keep the ale coming!'

From that time on, we seemed to be playing every night either for our lads or at other camps on the island. We enjoyed it immensely and we never had to buy any beer. We also had visits from members of ENSA who came to entertain us, and then we in turn entertained them in the mess and a good time was had by all.

We had a good crowd of officers who weren't averse to coming to our mess in the evenings and joining in some of the entertainment, and altogether life seemed quite enjoyable. We seemed remote from the war, our living quarters were comfortable and warm, and we had plenty to eat and drink. Quite a number of us, on being drafted to Scapa, thought at first that we would be able to save some money as life would be pretty quiet. How wrong we were!

Then came VE day. Our delight in the end of hostilities in Europe was tinged with regret that our days up at Scapa were numbered and we would soon be returned to our respective home depots. On 4 July 1945, two months after the end of hostilities, the base was closed and I said goodbye to all my friends and took the long ride back down to Chatham and eventually Cookham.

Life was just the same but with a new innovation. This was in the shape of a town patrol to be provided by the personnel from the camp. Normally this was carried out by the disciplinary staff in the main barracks, but they decided that Cookham Camp personnel should provide their own town patrol of one petty officer and two men.

The day it was first introduced caused a panic because the dress for this duty was uniform plus belt and gaiters, and gaiters could not be worn with ordinary shoes. The first people to be detailed for this duty tried wearing gaiters on top of shoes but there was a hole between the bottom of the gaiter and the top of the shoe displaying a view of the wearer's socks. They were immediately sent back by the inspecting officer with instructions to appear in the proper rig, that is, boots, and had to scour the camp in order to try and borrow a pair. They were successful to a minor degree, but one man had a pair which was a size too small and was nearly crippled by the time he finished, while another had a pair two sizes too big, and they almost fell off several times. An emergency meeting was called and it was decided to have a kitty to buy a few pairs of boots for the exclusive use of those detailed for town patrol; they were mostly size eight but one or two sevens and nines to suit all tastes.

We soon got the job well organised. We found a friendly pub run by an ex-matelot where there was a small room set aside for the exclusive use of patrols so that they could rest awhile and become suitably refreshed as required. There was also a dance hall that we visited near closing time in which we were always given a pint by the manager in order to see that the crowd left in an orderly manner when requested to do so.

In charge of the patrol from the main barracks was a warrant officer with whom we had to rendezvous at a specified time at the junction of Chatham and Rochester High Streets in order to prove that we were providing a patrol as instructed. One night when I was in charge of our patrol, we were approaching this rendezvous when we came across a Dutch seaman lying on the pavement. His mate was standing nearby leaning on a wall, smoking a fag and apparently quite unconcerned. Just then the barracks patrol plus warrant officer loomed up. The WO said, 'Hello, what have we here?' in the time-honoured manner.

I replied that it appeared to be a Dutch seaman but that we had no jurisdiction over other Allied forces, and what did he think we ought to do.

'Keep an eye on him,' said the WO. 'I'll go and get someone to sort this lot out.' Then he about turned and marched off. We stood there chatting for a few minutes, when suddenly the previously prone seaman got to his feet and he and his mate staggered off into the night. Some time later the WO and his patrol returned and immediately wanted to know where the recumbent body had disappeared to.

'He just got up and walked away, sir,' I replied.

The WO said, 'I thought I told you to keep an eye on him.'

'I did keep an eye on him and watched him walk away,' I told him. 'He wasn't committing an offence. He was just lying down. Maybe he was tired.'

The WO then gave a kind of a snort and said, 'Oh, bugger it!' He then turned about and vanished into the darkness, along with his cohorts.

London was less than an hour in the train from Chatham, and a couple of friends, Norman Hook and a PO telegraphist named Andy (I can't recall his full name), decided that it might be a good idea to go to the big city and see a show. We duly set off and on arrival, after having a meal, we went into a pub for a pint to pass the time until it was time to seek out a theatre. No sooner had we sat down than three pints appeared on the table bought by one of the people sitting in the pub. Naturally we returned the favour, but before we knew where we were three more pints were sent over – and so it went on until closing time arrived. We then staggered back to our bed and breakfast billet and caught the workmen's train back to Chatham in the morning.

A few days later we again decided that we would make another foray up to the city and see a show. We had the meal but avoided the pub that was responsible for us missing out and went into another one, but the same thing happened. Closing time saw us staggering back to our billet, minus a show! We made quite a few attempts to patronise the arts but with scant success. Those cockneys were a very kind-hearted people and we couldn't throw their kindness in their faces, could we?

Hostilities had ended in Europe and it seemed that the Japanese were not enjoying any more success out in the Far East. In fact, it has been said that they knew all was lost as far back as May 1945 and were endeavouring to find a way to effect some sort of surrender without losing face. Unfortunately, President Trueman was unaware of this and ordered the dropping of the atomic bomb on Hiroshima on 6 August followed by an ultimatum. Inexplicably, the Japanese ignored this ultimatum and so another bomb was released on Nagasaki on 9 August, with the result that the Japanese surrendered on 14 August 1945.

Naturally everyone was delighted that at last peace was with us once more and life could, in time, revert to normality. In Cookham, however, there were mixed feelings. Here we had a place full of people who were only in it because of the war, and now the war was over they all wanted out, straight away. They didn't want to know any more about the Navy or about discipline or about signals. They wanted to get back home to their families and jobs. They didn't want to hang about. They had done their bit for King and country and wanted to be on their way without delay. Unfortunately, this was not to be. The service doesn't work like that. Rosters had to be worked out. Procedures had to be observed, and it looked as though it might be months before some of these poor unfortunates would be demobbed.

To make matters worse, the officers in charge decreed that instructions would carry on just as normal at Cookham. Fleet manoeuvres and fleet dispositions that had proved absolutely useless in modern warfare still had to be taught. Morse and semaphore exercises still had to be read. Operating procedures and codes had to be learned and all this to people who were not the slightest bit interested and had no intention of assimilating any of the knowledge that we were told to impart. What a soul-destroying task!

Life could not go on in this fashion. I still had four years to do and didn't intend to endure four years of this sort of existence. It was time I got out and tried my luck in Civvy Street before all the jobs got snapped up by the hordes of people being demobbed every day.

I had a chum who was a PO sickbay tiffy, so had a word with him and he came up with the idea that I could be honourably discharged for being below naval physical standard with defective vision, plus the fact that I might be able to wangle a pension. He arranged for me to see the Base Medical Officer, who immediately pronounced me unfit to carry on in my present rate and told me I would have to be (regrettably) invalided out of the service. Within days the necessary papers were prepared, and on 26 April 1946 I packed my bag for the last time and became a civilian.

I have had some good times in the service and I've had some bad ones. If given the chance to do it all again, I very much doubt if I would. I really wanted an academic or musical career, but who knows what happens to folk in those careers in times of war? I must say I was glad to be in the Navy at the outbreak of hostilities. It is the service I would have chosen if called up, but one doesn't always get what one wants when it comes to service life; in fact, this happens very very rarely.

The ships in which I served have long ago ended their existence at the hands of the breakers, with the exception of the *Warspite*. It was as though she did not want to end her life in such an ignominious fashion. On the way to the breakers yard, she broke away from her tow off the Cornish coast at Marazion and ran aground on the rocks. All attempts to tow her off were resisted – a fighting ship to the end.

The Navy, as I knew it, has gone. The rot started with the abolition of the tot. The battlecruiser, the battleship and the cruiser have long since ceased to exist and have been superseded by the frigate and the destroyer of no more than 5,000 tons – but far more deadly. The mighty fifteen- and sixteen-inch guns have been replaced by the missile, which is more accurate and destructive.

Flag signals, Morse and semaphore are a thing of the past. Computers and electronics reign supreme and it seems that instead of Jolly Jack Tars the Navy is run by boffins and technicians. Time marches on. It is no good pining over the past; we have to look to the future, although sometimes I feel sorry for the matelot of today. He will never have some of the experiences that I and my shipmates often enjoyed.

18348009R00052

Printed in Great Britain
by Amazon